THE LADY IN THE BAY WINDOW

A true story of a haunted Sheffield home

William C. Grave

THANK YOU...

Before you embark on the captivating journey within these pages, I would like to take a moment to express my deepest gratitude to the remarkable individuals who have played an instrumental role in bringing this book to life.

First and foremost, my heartfelt thanks go to my Dad. From the moment I completed the first draft, he dedicated countless hours sitting by my side to help me reach my goal of finishing the book. His insights, guidance, and patience have been invaluable throughout this entire process. I cannot thank him enough for his support and belief in me.

Despite her own health challenges, my mum always managed to offer her voice from the living room couch when both my dad and I stumbled upon a tricky word or phrase. Her assistance brought a sense of warmth and encouragement, and for that, I am truly grateful.

To my close family members and friends, I extend my sincere appreciation. Your unwavering support, as you read the drafts and provided valuable feedback, has shaped this book into what it is today. Your input and constructive criticism have guided me on this journey, and I am humbled by your contributions.

A special thank you goes to Adrian Finney, the host of Strange Sheffield Ghost Walks and author of The Strange Britain Books. Adrian's expertise and creativity were instrumental in crafting the fantastic book cover that now graces these pages. I encourage you to explore his own works, as they are a great source of inspiration that drove me to pen my own story.

I would also like to express my gratitude to Tim Doyle, a psychic medium who played a pivotal role in providing insights during a house reading. His guidance and connection with the spiritual realm added depth to the narrative and brought a sense of authenticity to the book.

Furthermore, I extend my thanks to the team from Awakening the Paranormal, who dedicated their time to conduct a full investigation at my home. Their expertise and commitment to their craft enriched the storytelling experience and added an extra layer of intrigue.

Lastly, I want to thank you, the reader for purchasing my book. It brings me immense joy to inform you that all profits from book sales will be directed to Cavendish Cancer Care, a phenomenal local charity that provides vital support to those in need on a daily basis. Your support enables their noble mission, and together, we can bring hope and comfort to those facing the challenges of cancer.

INTRODUCTION

For the past 18 years I've been living in a house that is haunted.

Over time, I've experienced and witnessed numerous unexplainable occurrences, as have my family and friends who have visited or lived in my home with me. Despite my natural inclination towards rational explanations, I've been unable to dismiss these eerie happenings as mere coincidence or imagination. As a result, I've become increasingly curious about the paranormal, and I've embarked on a journey to document my experiences and those of others who have encountered inexplicable events in my home.

This book comprises 25 short stories, each is written about a true event that occurred in my house, in chronological order. While some might consider me sceptical, my experiences have convinced me that there are forces beyond our understanding at work in the world. However, I'm not here to convince anyone of anything, but to share my story and raise awareness for a cause close to my heart.

As a family member of a cancer sufferer, I often

feel helpless. My mum has had a rare incurable cancer for five years, and watching her struggle is heart-wrenching. Writing this book is my way of doing something to help, while keeping my mind busy. All proceeds from the book will go to a local cancer charity, with the hope of providing support to families who are suffering from this awful disease.

To protect the identities of those involved, I've changed the majority of the names and locations in this book. Although I'm not a professional writer, I felt compelled to share my story and contribute to a cause that means so much to me. This book is my tribute to my mother, who has always encouraged me to follow my passions and make a difference in the world. I hope you enjoy reading it as much as I enjoyed writing it.

CHAPTER 1

2004 was a crazy year to say the least. I was 19 at the time and pretty-happy-go-lucky, having little in the way of serious commitments. One that I did have, however, was to my fiancée. Together we'd decided to buy a house and were looking at places on the south side of Sheffield.

The truth is that I was still more than comfortable living at home with my parents. I'd just passed my apprenticeship at a local car retailer and had been promoted to the sales department, and at that time you could earn a pretty penny in car sales. My fiancée would frequently tell me that I should be spending my new-found wealth on something worthwhile… like a house. I didn't have any better ideas, so we started searching for our first home.

My life was simple back then. Mum would provide meals when required and I never had to think about washing and ironing my clothes, they just magically appeared in my room ready to wear. My dad was easy to get on with and had just retired early from a career in banking at the age of fifty.

All in all, I wasn't in a rush, but guided by my fiancée, we kept looking. We looked at a few houses around Charnock, a fairly desirable residential area on the southern edge of Sheffield. A house did come up that we both liked the look of but unfortunately the owner pulled out of the deal before the contracts had been exchanged, so we had to start searching again.

The next day my fiancée called me at work saying that another property had gone on the market in the same area. She couldn't wait to see it and asked if I could book in for a viewing that weekend.

I drove to the house on the Friday just to have a quick look from the outside. It was a semi-detached property situated quite high up from the roadside. The house was brick-built, and the bricks looked dark and weatherworn. It had two large bay windows, one above the other, that overlooked the front garden, and a much smaller window above the front door to the right of the house. All the windows and frames looked like they needed replacing. There were two overgrown hedges running down either side, the one to the left was very tall and bordered the adjoining semi-detached house next door. The one to the right ran alongside a steep, pitted stone path that led up to the front door. I couldn't see much more from the car because there was another tall hedge atop a brick wall which came right out to the roadside pavement. Although the house must have seen better days my first thoughts were that it had potential. I didn't feel comfortable going any closer uninvited, so I gave the house one last look before driving away. I was looking forward to telling my fiancée about it and eagerly awaited the viewing the next day. I had a restless night's sleep, excited but also a little apprehensive at the prospect of becoming a homeowner and taking on new responsibilities for the first time.

The following morning, we pulled up outside the house and I asked her what her first thoughts were. She was beaming and couldn't wait to go inside. As we walked up the steep path, we passed an ancient looking sundial on the left, in the centre of a paved garden. I hadn't seen this feature on my first visit as it was hidden behind the walled hedge. The viewing went well. It had a fairly spacious lounge, three bedrooms, two bathrooms and a newly installed kitchen. The master bedroom was a good size and the bedroom at the back of the house was suitable for a double bed. The third bedroom was more of a boxroom but could sleep one person at a push. The ceilings were very high and the whole house had just been refurbished in very neutral colours, so it all looked brand spanking new, on the inside at least. There was a fairly large back garden that was accessed via the kitchen and the attached lean-to utility room. When I say lean-to, I really mean lean-to, as it looked like it could collapse at any moment. There were cracked panes and the roof leaked, with several tiles broken or missing completely. The utility room housed the washing machine, dryer and WC. The outside of the house needed some major repairs, but the inside was very homely. All that considered, we both thought this was the house, we had to have it.

We were ecstatic to find that our offer was accepted very quickly and that we should have a date for moving in within a couple of months. Things seemed to be happening at an alarmingly fast pace. Could it really be this easy to buy a house?

A few weeks passed, and on a cold, dark December night I was getting ready to go out on a Christmas do with my work colleagues. We were going ten-pin bowling followed by a night on the town. I was sitting in my mum and dad's living room, waiting for Craig to come and pick me up. Craig was not only a work colleague but a very good friend. He'd shaved his head to hide his receding hairline and always had the remnants of oil smears on his hands from his job as a car mechanic.

It was 8pm and Craig arrived in his souped-up Vauxhall Corsa. I knew it was his car coming up the road before I laid eyes on it because of the noisy, over-the-top exhaust. The cars blue, 'illegal', side lights shimmered through the front window of my mum and dad's house as he pulled up outside.

I got in the car and as he drove down the road, I excitedly told him that I'd just bought my first house and that I'd be moving in with my fiancée before the end of the year. He asked where it was, and I told him it was only around the corner, about five minutes' drive away. Craig was quick to respond, 'Let's go and have a look before we go to the bowling alley.'

We soon arrived at the house and I looked out of the passenger window. 'It's that one there, buddy.' I said.

Craig parked up, leant across and ducked his head so he could get a better view of the house.
'Nice, it looks like a lovely place. Who's the old lady in the bay window?' he asked.
I stared at the house. The windows were empty. The house was empty... or should have been!
I turned to him, 'What old lady?'
He raised his arm past my chest and pointed an oil-stained finger at the upper bay window.
'There! In the top window, that old lady staring down at us.'
I looked again. There was no one there.
'Are you sure you're looking at the right house, it's number 333?'
Craig ducked once again, knowing he'd have to stretch his neck to see, as the house stood very high above the road.

'I'm certain Will, she's looking at us now, you must be able to see her?'

All I could see was an empty house, there weren't even any curtains up. To me, there was nothing there to be seen.

Craig shrugged his shoulders as he started to drive away. As we set off I wondered what the hell had just happened. Was he kidding me? If not, what on earth had he really seen? I couldn't just let it go and quizzed him on what he'd supposedly seen.

'What did this so-called old woman look like?' Craig, looking more convincing than ever replied, 'She was quite a small old lady, probably in her eighties. She was wearing a darkish coloured cardigan over a white blouse. She had short, grey, permed hair and quite a piercing stare. Her arms were straight and leaning on the window ledge of the bay window upstairs, almost like she didn't look happy with us parking outside her house. She was looking right at us.'
He was so convincing with his description that it played on my mind for the rest of the journey.

It seems strange looking back at this incident that I didn't really ask much more at the time. I didn't think he was being serious. I thought he was just joking around, trying to scare me. It didn't scare me at all as I didn't see anything. Little did I know that this…the first sighting of many, would come back to haunt me.

CHAPTER 2

It was now December 18th, 2004, the day I finally got the keys to my new home.

I was a 19-year-old lad, about to flee the nest from my mum and dad's. What was I thinking? I didn't even know how to make pasta and sauce. How would I survive at my new place, when my fiancée, to be fair, was even less domesticated than me?

I spent the morning gathering my belongings from my mum and dad's, which at the time weren't much to behold...a 28-inch widescreen television, a couple of pillows, a duvet, my games console and an open mind. My current car was a 2004 red Volkswagen beetle cabriolet (I know - not the manliest of cars). I had so few belongings at the time, I managed to move house in a beetle cabriolet.

I drove to the estate agents just up the road and picked up the keys to the house. The lady at the estate agents assured me that the previous owners would be well gone by the time I got to the property. They'd been told to vacate by 12 noon, and it was now almost 1pm.

The house had been vacant since the previous

owner purchased it for his mother. She hadn't taken to the property and wanted to move out after only two months. Her son had spent the following four months refurbishing the interior of the house before I bought the property in November of 2004. I knew nothing of any owners before this as I hadn't seen or spoken with them during the purchase.

I rolled up in my little red Beetle cabriolet and pulled up outside my new home. I stared up the steep path, took a deep breath and thought, this is it. The reality of moving out hit me. I felt excited but slightly nauseous as the keys to the front door jangled in my hand. I turned the key in the door and stopped for a second. I could hear movement in the house. I walked through the door to confront whomever or whatever was in my home.

A large, muscular, bald-headed man greeted me in the front room as I opened the door from the hallway.

'I'm Nick,' he said. 'Nice to meet you, you must be William? I'm so sorry we couldn't leave before you arrived. I've just nipped in to pick up the last of my tools after fitting a new kitchen for you.' Before I had a chance to say anything, Nick's huge figure moved to one side and a small, well-dressed lady with long dark hair approached me and shook my hand.

'I'm Nick's mum, I was living here. He bought it from an estate auction six months ago. The previous old lady had the house from new in the 1930's when it was a council house, but sadly passed away. Nick bought it for me, but I only lasted two months here.' Then she moved a bit closer and whispered under her breath to me, 'Something just wasn't right.' It was almost like she didn't want her son to hear.

He heard and bellowed out, 'MOTHER! don't scare the young lad, it's his first home. You'll be fine here buddy, don't listen to her. Anyway, we'll get out of your hair and let you settle in.' And just like that they were gone. I didn't even get a chance to ask what she meant when she said, 'something wasn't right'.

I walked around the house on the old, original floorboards to marvel at what I was going to do going forward. How would I decorate the place? What carpets would I lay, or would I sand down the beautiful, oak floorboards? The floorboards had been varnished with a dark mahogany colour. You could see where the rugs used to lie on the floor, as somebody had varnished around them.

I still didn't put two and two together. A work colleague/friend had seen an old lady. I'm being warned by the previous owner, a lovely old lady, who found the house too unsettling to live in. What was I in for in the coming days?

CHAPTER 3

It was the first night in my new pad, right after the second warning shot from the previous owner's mum.

My fiancée at the time didn't want to move in until we had carpets, beds and furniture. I on the other hand couldn't wait, so like a giddy kid I invited a few of the lads round to see my new place that evening.

They arrived in their droves in various taxis around 7pm with a crate of beer under one arm and a sleeping bag or duvet under the other. We were going to see the first night in, in style.

As the lads entered one by one, they walked straight into the kitchen and put their beer in the fridge ready for the night ahead. We chatted away for a while before embarking on a grand tour of the house. After I'd shown them round we headed back downstairs to the living room. The room was a decent size, with an original fireplace that had been bricked up and then tiled over with some fancy, floral tiles. The walls were painted in a beige colour with a picture rail three quarters of the way up each wall and coving marrying the walls to the ceiling. The large bay window at the front of the house dominated the front room especially as there were no curtains. On the far side to the left was a small alcove that was set back into the wall, and two doors to exit either to the kitchen or the hallway. The previous owner, Nick, had tried his best to modernise the house whilst keeping all its charming features during the refurbishment.

I hadn't even sorted a TV licence out and being young and naive, didn't want to risk putting the TV on for fear of being fined. I'd borrowed the original 'Monopoly' board game from my parents and all six of us made makeshift seats from our duvets and sleeping bags. We were ready to drink the night away and play the long and arduous game of 'Monopoly' in the middle of the room where the rug once laid.

It was Christmas time, so I'd bought a small, cheap, Christmas tree and decorated it to go in the alcove in the front room. As we played and drank, the tree stood there twinkling its lights looking very out of place.

A few beers in and a good two hours into the board game, my friend, Greg, who was sitting with his back facing the alcove, looked over his shoulder, and suddenly yelled out in fear. In a panic, he scrambled across the board, knocking drinks, hotels, houses, cards and playing pieces all over the place. He then sat shaking against the wall and didn't say anything but stared at where the tree had been placed under the alcove.

There was anger in the air as two hours of 'Monopoly' had been ruined, and people's drinks had been spilled but still Greg sat, shaking, with his hands tucked over his legs in a foetal position against the wall.

'What the hell happened?' I asked. Still nothing, just a petrified look on his face and his eyes bulging out of his head in fear.

I grabbed Greg and took him in the kitchen to calm him down and have a chat. All he said was, 'Did you not see her? She was right there, an old lady sitting on an invisible chair next to the Christmas tree, just staring at me...hovering on nothing.'

Greg was a tall, strapping lad and, put it this way, you wouldn't mess with him. For him to be scared was a first for me to see. He's also the kind of guy who wouldn't lie about something like this, we had known each other since we were eleven.

'What did the lady look like?' I asked. With a panic in his voice, he shrieked back at me, 'She was an old lady, probably in her 80's/90's, with short curly, grey hair, a long dark skirt, white blouse and a dark-coloured cardigan. She was staring straight at me.' It took a good hour or so of drinking and talking with the lads to calm Greg down, and a hell of a lot more drinking for him to stay the night. We all slept on the floor in the front room that night.

I'm not going to lie, I'm kind of glad I wasn't home alone. Or would I have been?

I'm now starting to piece together the three things that had happened in the last week.

First there was the sighting of the old lady looking out of the bedroom window by Craig. Then the quiet warning I got from the previous owner telling me that she didn't feel right about the house. Lastly Greg's frightening experience seeing the old lady materialise right in front of him.

Bearing in mind that I hadn't mentioned a word to Greg about the first two incidents, and the fact that he didn't know my work colleague Craig, they couldn't possibly have spoken prior to the scary event that night.

CHAPTER 4

I'd been in the house for four weeks now and there was nothing new to report on the paranormal front.

The house was starting to look like a home. We'd had cream carpets fitted throughout most of the house (not a sensible choice for teenage house owners). The back bedroom and the living room, where I'd painstakingly sanded down and varnished the original oak floorboards, were the only rooms without carpets. We had a king-size bed in the master bedroom and furniture to match.

Downstairs was starting to look more homely too, after purchasing two 2-seater settees, a pouffe to put your feet on and a stand for the old widescreen TV.

After many weeks of internal decorating it was time to tackle the outside of the house. The back garden looked very neglected and was knee high in weeds and surrounded by overgrown hedges. My mission was to turn this jungle of a garden into something respectable.

I was standing on the back garden one morning

contemplating where to start, when I heard somebody open the back door of the neighbouring house. This wasn't the semi-detached house attached to mine; it was the next one down the road, which belonged to a lovely old chap I came to know as Tezza.

Tezza was probably in his late seventies. He had short swept over grey hair, and was quite short and stocky. We'd crossed paths on a few occasions as he regularly visited the local pub up the road. Tezza was a lovely man who'd always stop to have a chat, and he had a really positive spin on life. He was a little unsteady on his feet especially on his way back from the pub. Tezza walked out of the back of his house and spotted me having a look at the garden. He smiled, 'Looks like you've got your work cut out there' he then said. His own garden was very well kept and was the exact opposite of mine. I agreed and thought I'd take this opportunity to subtly ask about my house and find out if he knew anything about the previous owners.

Tezza peered over the untidy hedge, 'I knew the old lady who'd lived there for years. I believe she'd been in the house from when it was new in the 1930's. Lovely old lady, always very smartly dressed and spoke very posh too.' I hesitated but plucked up the courage to ask… 'Has anyone ever mentioned anything strange happening in the house?' He looked a bit bemused and asked me what I meant by this.

At this point I'm on the fence with the whole thing. Do I ask if it's haunted? Am I just being daft? Should I just leave it? Nothing has happened in the past month, perhaps Craig and the old lady (Nick's mum) were winding me up. Had Greg misinterpreted what he'd seen? I looked Tezza in the eyes and proceeded with my question, 'has anyone seen anything, you know… like anything unnatural, like a ghost or anything?'

Tezza laughed, 'Not to my knowledge, although if anyone was going to haunt the house it would be Mrs. Tompkins, the lady I was telling you about. She loved the place, took great pride in making sure the garden was always immaculately kept. She'd clean the place every day, the windows were always gleaming. Bless her, she passed away a few years ago through old age.'

I didn't know what else to say, I'm now thinking the sightings could be real. The beauty of it is, it sounded like Mrs. Tompkins loved this house as much as I did. I just hoped she wasn't mad at the fact that I was living here now. I'd made some changes to the place, and this was now my home.

Since this chat in the winter of early 2005, Tezza, as he was known to me and my mates, has sadly passed away. He was a gentleman and is truly missed. He left his home to his lovely daughter

and her husband who live there to this day. His daughter Claire has helped me gain a better picture of Mrs. Tompkins through my research for this book.

The house was built as a council house and completed on the 25th of March 1936, or at least that's the date that the lady we speak of, moved in. Mrs. Tompkins was a very well to do lady, as Tezza had mentioned. She was always smartly dressed, spoke very posh and was always polite. These attributes would have suited her well because she worked as a furrier, dealing in expensive fur coats. She had a partner for many years, until her other half sadly passed away in the house. We don't know if Mrs. Tompkins spent her last moments in her beloved home, but we certainly think she visits here from time to time.

CHAPTER 5

It had now been six months living in my new home. The relationship with my fiancée didn't work out and we decided to go our separate ways. I was living alone in a three bed, semi-detached house, which was potentially haunted.

I decided to put a message out to a few good friends of mine to see if they were interested in renting the two spare rooms. It wasn't easy being a single 19-year-old, trying to keep on top of the bills and burn the candle at both ends going out with the lads every weekend.

One of my oldest friends Doug responded to my message, and seemed very interested in moving in. We were best of mates growing up, as my older brother and his brother played football together. We'd effectively known each other from the age of six. We lost touch a little when we went to different schools at the age of eleven, but still saw each other out and about every now and then. I invited Doug round to have a look at what would potentially be his new shared pad.

Doug was a real good lad, medium build with mousey coloured, messy hair. We'd been on many an adventure as young lads growing up together. He was always up for a challenge, and was currently doing an apprenticeship as an electrician and fancied moving out to get a bit of independence in his life. Doug arrived on a Saturday morning and I greeted him at the front door as he walked up the steep path to the front of the house. We sat and had a beer and a catch-up in the front room before I showed him his potential new bedroom.

The second bedroom overlooked the once overgrown rear garden and had a view to the tram stop in the distance at Gleadless Townend. The room itself was completely empty and the smell of freshly sanded floorboards and newly eggshell-painted walls hit you as soon as you entered. It was a decent sized room made to look larger by the staggering height of the ceilings. It looked more modern than other rooms in the house as it was the only room that didn't have a picture rail. Doug took one look and said, 'I can see myself in here, love it! When can I move in?'

We ventured back downstairs and agreed terms for him to move in as soon as possible. I asked if he knew anybody else who might fancy renting the box room. He told me about a good friend of his from the first school we went to together. Doug was only two months younger than me, but this meant he fell into the year below at school. At the time I didn't know the lad he was talking about.

Within hours I was being introduced to Dan who would become my best pal for the coming years. He was a very skinny, tall guy with blonde spikey hair and he wouldn't mind me saying this, but he had a rather large nose. He seemed a very genuine lad from the off and I was happy to show him the box room. The box room, or third bedroom, was small, hence the name. It was the only room which didn't have central heating but had enough space for a single bed and space to put clothes and other odds and sods. Dan also really wanted to move out of his family home and after discussing the ridiculously low room rate (it was the box room, with no heating after all), he agreed to move in.

In the coming weeks both lads bought a bed and moved their meagre belongings into their respective rooms. There were now three of us living here and the house was full of laughter and good times.

I left it a few days, before one night, drunkenly telling the lads about the events that had occurred in the weeks leading up to me moving in. It didn't scare them one bit. If anything they were both intrigued by the whole situation. Doug then asked me what I kept in the loft. The old wooden, two-foot square loft hatch was the first thing you would see, five feet above your head, as you walked out onto the landing from his bedroom. I replied, 'Actually I've never been up there. I've not even accumulated enough things to fill the house, never mind needing space in the loft.'

That was it, three drunken lads decided it was a good idea at 10pm, to attempt to get into a loft hatch on a ten-foot-high ceiling, without ladders, to see what was up there. We were going to draw straws to see who went up but Doug said he wanted to do it. Besides, Dan and I were taller and it would be easier for us to throw him up there by hand. We didn't have a torch but Doug had his old flip-mobile phone which could emit a small light, so we were good to go.

I stood with my back against Doug's bedroom door and clasped my hands together, in order to hitch Doug up to ceiling height. He managed to reach the loft hatch and carefully pushed the heavy wooden hatch door up. It made an eerie grating noise as he slid it back across the loft floor. We could now see into a dark void in the ceiling. It was pitch black. Dan then stood alongside me, grabbed Doug's other foot and proceeded to push him up into the darkness of the loft. As his head reached the entrance, he asked us to stop for a second so he could pan his light around and see what was there. He suddenly threw his phone to the ground and kicked at us both, before falling to the ground shrieking, 'What the hell is that?'

Dan and I looked at Doug excitedly, hollering simultaneously, 'Why, what did you see?'

Doug, looking unnerved said, 'There's a bloody, old looking stool, right in the centre of the room. Nothing but darkness, dust, cobwebs and a tiny ancient looking stool. It's right in the middle of the room. How weird is that?' And without further ado, he wanted to go back up, sit on the stool and video around the room to see if anything, or anyone, was up there with him.

I was against the idea at first. After all, this was my home and I'd had a few weird things happen already. I didn't want to wake something up that didn't want to be woken. Doug insisted that he wanted to do it and eventually I folded... Dan and I were, once again, pushing Doug up by his feet into the void. To make it spookier, Doug closed the heavy loft hatch on himself and walked to the centre of the large loft space. He took a good look at the stool, before wiping the surface and taking a seat, with his flip-phone camera light in hand. It was pitch black up there and the light was all but useless.

The stool was no more than a foot tall with a rich mahogany frame and four spindle hand-crafted legs. It had a dark green, leather seat that looked a bit like a saddle and large brass studs pinning the leather to the mahogany frame. The seat looked about a hundred years old at least, yet there it was, plonked right in the centre of my loft space surrounded by nothing but darkness.

Dan and I anxiously giggled to each other at the top of the landing, 'Rather him than me', Dan joked. We could hear the nervous voice of Doug, asking if anyone was up there with him, and if there was, could they show themselves to the light on his dodgy phone camera.

A few minutes passed in silence, then came the grating sound of the loft hatch slowly opening. Doug's head suddenly appeared... 'Get me out of here! I'm done!' he shouted.

Doug brought the stool down with him and we now understood why he was so concerned in the first place. This was a mighty creepy item.

We regrouped in the front room over a beer or two and questioned why this creepy stool was left there. Was it a joke, or did it have meaning? I secretly hoped that I wouldn't find out.

This was the hardest story to write. As I mentioned, Dan was my best pal for the years to come. He was a real diamond of a lad that would do anything for anyone and we could talk for hours. He'd always keep you intrigued about what he was going to say next. His laugh sounded like a braying donkey, and he'd have us all in stitches. Not a day goes by that I don't think about my pal, Daniel Backhouse (AKA Captain). He lost his life too soon, at the tender age of

twenty-two.

A few weeks after this event the video of Doug's brave attempt, sitting in the loft alone on the mysterious stool, had been watched by several of the lads we knew. The majority thought he was either crackers or just brave. A good friend, Brunden, noticed on the pixelated video, that there were several white light anomalies or orbs, as they are known in the spiritual world. These orbs usually appear when a bright light, such as the torch on Doug's phone are capturing an image. Some say that these are spirits trying to manifest. Sceptics say it's just dust caught in the lens flare of the camera. All I know is that the catchphrase, 'There were bare orbs in that video', was bandied around our circle of friends for the coming weeks.

CHAPTER 6

I'd been in the house for over two years now and was in my glory days as a fresh faced, twenty-one year old. It was now a regular occurrence for me and other house guests to hear heavy footsteps around the house when nobody was there. Doors would open and close by themselves when there was no draught or windows open. People had also seen the odd dark shadow move slowly across gaps under doorways, when there was nobody on the other side of the door.

I had quite a large circle of friends, the majority from my school days. Pretty much everybody who had been in the house had now witnessed a paranormal event. I mean this in the sense of something happening that no one can explain.

I worked seventy to eighty hours a week now as a fully-fledged salesperson at the same main car dealer that I'd started with as an apprentice six years ago. When I did get a weekend off I enjoyed my Saturdays doing three of my favourite things; having the lads round, drinking and watching the football on TV. One particular Saturday was a bit of a special one as the Manchester derby was on for the late kick off at 5.30pm.

Doug and Dan were already with me, we'd been vegetating in the living room all day with a can of beer in hand. We chewed the fat amongst ourselves whilst watching the football results come in.

The first of our evening guests to arrive was Ben, a good pal of mine who was quite short and stocky with mousey, thinning, short hair and thick, milk-bottle-lensed glasses. Ben was always outspoken and loved a loud debate. Brad was next to arrive. He was a real character with long, dark-brown, rocker-style hair. He was a fantastic musician too and could play the guitar and drums. He often brought his guitar round to show us his skills. The last to arrive was Bungle, nicknamed after the popular children's TV character from 'Rainbow'. He looked the spitting image, similar height and build and even had the curly, short hair to match. Every group of friends had a Bungle, 99% of what he said wasn't true, but his ramblings were so entertaining to listen to you'd never question his stories.

Bungle returned from the kitchen with a beer for all six of us and sat on one of the two-seater sofas next to Ben. The sofa they were on was situated in the bay window to the right of the TV. Brad was perched on the arm of their sofa whilst Doug, Dan and I were squeezed on the other sofa facing the TV, with our three sets of feet on the pouffe.

The big Saturday night football game had kicked off and we were enjoying a much-needed lads' night in. I was talking to Brad about his band's latest gig, when suddenly something happened.

The sofa that I was on suddenly lifted on a tilt at the end I was sitting, then it crashed back down with a huge bang onto the wooden floorboards. Brad's eyes were as wide as saucers and he'd gone deathly pale. There was an eerie silence in the room. 'What the hell was that?' I yelled.

Brad shakily replied, 'I've just seen what happened. The sofa you guys were sitting on lifted a good five inches into the air at one end and then fell back to the floor!'

Bungle and Ben looked worried. They obviously heard the loud bang but didn't see it as they were facing the other way watching the football. I tried to appease Brad and get him a drink to calm him down but he was having none of it. He put the can of beer I'd offered him on the window ledge, turned to me as he put his jacket on and said, 'I'm serious mate, I'm going and never coming back here again, that's not normal!' And just like that he walked out.

Doug and Dan had also felt the sofa lift; it was an impossible feat. All three of us had had our feet up on the large pouffe in the middle of the room. The sofa itself was a large, heavy two-seater, with a wooden frame. Whatever force had caused it to lift must have been very strong and it certainly wasn't natural.

Brad was right. It wasn't normal, it was paranormal. We debated this for the rest of the evening. There was no explanation as to why the heavy sofa had lifted on its own and then slammed to the floor. Or was there?

It's now been 15 years since I've seen Brad. He used to come round to my house two or three times a week. True to his word he never returned and the haunted look on his face stays with me to this day.

CHAPTER 7

2008 was a dark year as the whole nation was plunged into a recession. It was an even darker year for my circle of friends as we lost one of our own. I'd been to many funerals in my time, the majority of which had been family members who had lived long happy lives; had a good innings, as us Yorkshire folk would say.

In early spring I'd be asked a huge favour by my brother, Darren. He'd been courting a new girlfriend for a while and they were set to wed later in the year. They were currently living in an apartment behind my mum and dad's house and had asked if I would move into the apartment, so they could live in my house. This would be a temporary arrangement until after the wedding, as they were looking for a place for themselves and needed more space.

This couldn't have come at a better time for me. The recession had sent the car trade into an absolute mess and the business I'd been with for eight years, had cut their wages by twenty percent. The only issue was, I was drowning. Dan and Doug had just moved out and on my reduced wage, I couldn't afford to live the life I wanted. I agreed to let my brother and his fiancée move into my house, and I took the short drive down the road to live at my parents' in the apartment behind their house.

My brother was huge back then. He was feared by many and at 6'2", 22 stone of muscle, tattooed up to the nines you'd understand why. Because of his demeanour he always seemed to bring trouble his way and was often in fights, be that on a football pitch at a weekend or out downtown. He loved a drink too, spending most of his weekends in the local sports and social club. He was the opposite of me. As the saying goes, 'I'm a lover not a fighter.'

Darren would often call me to keep me updated on the latest paranormal events in the house. He hated every one of them. For a big bloke the random footsteps, banging, and general noises around the house scared him to death.

By this point I'd settled in at the apartment at my mum and dad's and still saw the lads as they would often visit to play the latest soccer game on my games console. Sometimes we'd take a football onto the sports field up the road for a kick-about.

On the 10th of May my world was turned upside down when I got the phone call to tell me Dan was in hospital and it was critical. I drove to the hospital as soon as I got the news, but I was too late. My best pal had lost his fight to stay alive. I was a broken man. I was given the job of phoning close family and friends to break the news to them. I was sitting with tears rolling down my face outside the Accident and Emergency unit of the Northern General Hospital. I somehow managed to pull myself together just enough to drive back to my mum and dad's.

To get to the apartment around the back of their house you had to go through the garage by lifting the heavy metal door. I was often greeted by my mum, dad, or both as I drove on to the drive at the front of the house. Today it was my dad who popped his head around the front door and said, 'Are you ok? You look shocking.' As I lifted the garage door he could see straight away that I was far from ok. My dad took the time to speak with me as I broke down entering the apartment at the back of the house. I couldn't even speak. He put a hand on my shoulder as I stood, with one hand over my face and the other leant against the kitchen counter. He waited with me until I eventually sat down and said I needed some time alone. There was nothing anybody could say to console me.

Although we are a very close family, my brother and I avoided hugs once we started senior school. By this, I mean that our way of showing affection was usually in the form of a bit of banter. Laughter is of course the best medicine. As an adult, the first time I remember hugging my mum and dad was just outside the exit to the crematorium after Dan's funeral. They could see I was ruined and I

WILLIAM C. GRAVE

must say I needed it.

After this horrendous life event I turned myself into a bit of a recluse. I left my job to run a small used-car operation for a friend of mine and very rarely saw any of the lads. They all tried to contact me, but I was never in the right frame of mind.

I left my mum and dad's apartment and moved back into my house in the early winter that year. It had been eight months since I'd set foot in the place. It was a strange feeling as I walked into the front room and was greeted by a new brown leather three-seater sofa on the back wall and a matching single armchair, tucked neatly in the bay window. Something didn't feel right. There seemed to be a presence in the room with me. I'd often felt this just before something strange happened in the house, but this time it was stronger than ever. It felt like someone was beside me as I sat staring at the blank TV in front of me. It was so quiet, you could hear a pin drop. In that moment for some strange reason, I felt compelled to speak out.

'I can feel that you are here with me. Is that Dan or some other spirit in the house with me?' I nervously asked. I'd never done this before, why was I doing it now?

I grabbed my flip phone from my pocket and asked again, 'If you are here, I can feel you near me, can you show yourself in front of this camera?' I took a photo of what I could see in front of me, which was just the old TV. It wasn't switched on. On the right was the closed door leading to the bottom of the stairs.

I looked down at the image of the photo on my phone. The image quality wasn't the best but when I pressed the button to zoom in and take a closer look, I could see it. A large dark figure stood next to me reflected in the TV screen.

The feeling I first had, that Dan was in the room with me soon disappeared. This wasn't him. Dan was skinny and six-foot in stature. This was a taller, dark, shadowy figure standing next to me. It towered over me as I sat on the sofa. It stood with its arms by its side, almost like it was posing for the picture. You could see what I was wearing in the TV reflection, just jeans and a T-shirt. I also had a very concerned look on my face, but the figure next to me was just a black mass, with no detail at all. It had no facial features but a definite outline of a bulky looking guy.

I drove to my mum and dad's in shock and showed the image to them. They were amazed by what I had captured but just as baffled as me with the whole thing. In the coming weeks I showed it to a few friends too. As mates do, they ridiculed me about it and said there must have been someone standing there. There wasn't.

A few weeks after this, I went to a party at a friend of a friend's house, and my phone was stolen whilst it was on charge. I was devastated. Not only had the photo gone, but also all the text messages I'd received over the years from my pal Dan. Someone somewhere has an old 'Panasonic' flip phone with a very paranormal picture on it.

CHAPTER 8

A year had slipped by since my dear friend had passed away. I sat there on that day, the 10th of May, the anniversary of his death, the day that would never be the same again, and sank into a reflective mood. The silence was comforting as my thoughts wandered from memory to memory, recalling the face of someone who had left us forever. Every year on this day, I raise a glass to the lad we all knew as the 'Captain.'

I was getting my life back on track bit by bit and had truly settled back into my home. The economy was also getting back on its feet. I'd left the used car lot and re-joined the main car retailer that I'd worked for previously, this time as a Business Manager in Rotherham. Going back to a previous employer isn't usually the best move but this was a new position in a new place and something inside told me to grab the opportunity with both hands. It had begun well. I'd been given a lot of freedom to do things how I wanted and I was building an awesome team of great people around me. As everything started to slot together I felt that I could finally start to enjoy life again.

A couple of the lads had moved into the spare rooms too. Paul was a self-taught IT wizard. He was medium build, wore glasses and had a shaved head. He rented the larger room overlooking the rear garden and kitted out his room like something from a sci-fi movie. He had a homemade, large tower computer and two monitors atop a very impressive glass desk.

Matt, on the other hand, took the smaller box-room which looked out to the front of the house. He was a slightly larger lad with messy red hair. He got up very early every day to go to his job as a metal specialist. Matt suffered from OCD, but this wasn't a bad trait to have for a new roommate. He would insist on cleaning the house every day until it was spotless. His girlfriend, Carrie would often come round and stay with him over the weekend. I have no idea how they managed to fit in the tiny single bed in that room, but somehow, they did.
It was great to have the house full of laughter again. I'd known both of my new lodgers from the age of eleven and we all enjoyed a beer or three and socialising most evenings.

However, it was starting to feel like the norm for my brother to arrive at the front door on a Sunday afternoon. He'd always be three sheets to the wind after spending the morning playing football before heading to the sports and social club, until he could drink no more. This didn't go down well with his wife, so to avoid any arguments at home he'd arrive at my house around 5pm every Sunday to say he was stopping on the sofa.
I've mentioned before that we'd hear strange,

unexplained noises and shadows would be seen around the house, but one particular Sunday the house really came to life.

Matt, Paul, Darren, and I were all sat having a relaxing afternoon watching the TV, when my brother, who was in the armchair in the bay window suddenly shouted out for me to pause the TV. He was staring towards the bottom of the door to his right, where there was a visible gap as the carpets had been removed. It was dark and the door was closed, but you could see a bright light from the streetlamp outside reflecting onto the shiny, wooden floorboards beneath.

'What's wrong?' I blurted.

'I've just seen a shadow move slowly past the bottom of the door!'

Bearing in mind that my brother had previously lived in the house for eight months, this was the first time he'd seen this happen. He was clearly concerned as he nervously stroked his chin, exclaiming, 'This shouldn't be happening!'

We all heard the clearest footsteps we'd ever witnessed. The TV was still paused and there was no traffic noise from outside. The footsteps sounded like a heavy-footed person with boots on, walking slowly away from us up the staircase. The noise started to fade as the footsteps reached the landing at the top of the stairs. The loose floorboard on the hallway at the top of the stairs creaked, as the heavy-set figure made its way to the bathroom door. The tension was building as we sat motionless, listening, not daring to breathe. We clearly heard the doorknob turn, then the hinges of the door squeak as it opened and the footsteps began again as they made their way on to the tiled floor. The door then slammed shut and silence once again descended on the house as we all looked in astonishment at each other. We started to laugh as we sought to break the tension. Our masculine bravado kicked in and we started to joke about it.

'It looks like we're in for an interesting night,' quipped Paul, but the laughter was a little forced and the looks on our faces betrayed our anxiety.

'Someone's got to go and have a look,' said Matt, looking straight at me.
'Me?' I asked, sounding a little more afraid than I wanted.
'Well it's your house,' Paul chipped in.
'Yeah, go and have a look,' Darren agreed, 'We'll be here if you need us.'
'Oh great, marvellous. Thanks for that.'
They laughed as I crossed to the door and slowly pulled it open. As I made my way upstairs and onto the landing, I switched every light on along the way. I moved down the small upstairs hallway and checked every room, opening the doors with a show of confidence that I didn't really feel. There was no one there.

As I returned to the top of the stairs and reached the creaky floorboard I called out,
'If there's anyone there, please don't jump out on me!'
I heard nervous laughter from downstairs. I had no doubt they wouldn't be laughing if it was one of them in my place. I approached the bathroom door slowly and took the doorknob in my hand. I turned it. It made the same intense noise we'd heard only minutes ago. I pushed the door open, reached in and pulled on the light switch. To my relief there was nobody to be seen.

I arrived back at the bottom of the stairs. My brother then asked me to try and replicate the shadow under the door by standing behind it and closing it. I walked by slowly as he worryingly said, 'That's it! That's exactly what I saw but it was walking slower than you just did.'
I walked back into the front room, shrugging my shoulders in disbelief, as I re-joined the lads on the sofa.

Matt, Paul, and I were comfortable with what we had just witnessed, as this was a fairly regular occurrence. My brother wasn't. He was even contemplating facing the wrath of going home rather than sleeping downstairs alone.

We continued the evening, watching TV, discussing casually what had just happened. As time passed it seemed less and less real and we could discuss it in an ever more relaxed way.
Then suddenly Darren shouted, 'Pause it again!'

The heavy footsteps were back, pacing at the top of the stairs, backwards and forwards along the hallway. This second time really got to Darren.

'Stop this now!' he shouted at the ceiling, 'you're freaking me out!'

The noise suddenly stopped.

We held our breaths, straining to hear, but there were no more footsteps, no more sounds. It was like Darren had been heard and understood, as if whatever it was had no intention of scaring us and wanted to leave us in peace. We heard nothing more that night.

I'm no expert on all of this, these are just my experiences. I have just learnt to live with it when it happens. I admit that I am quite sceptical about the whole thing, but also have an open mind. I say I'm sceptical, but there are things that have happened that I just can't explain. These events don't happen all the time but tend to repeat every couple of months and continue for a few days after. The spirit/entity, whatever it is, then leaves me alone again for a month or two.

I've done some research into what the experts say about this sort of stuff happening, especially the footsteps. The experts in this field say there's such a thing called 'stone tape theory', which is the speculation that ghosts, and hauntings are likened to tape recordings. Mental impressions, during emotional or traumatic events, are thought to be projected in the form of energy and recorded onto rocks or other inanimate

objects. These can then be replayed under certain conditions. This kind of haunting is known as residual energy. The thing with residual energy is that the spirit or being wouldn't respond to what my brother said. This makes me think that we don't have residual energy. I believe there is at least one intelligent spirit in the house and this spirit/spirits doesn't seem to want to harm or upset us... yet.

CHAPTER 9

It was now 2012, and over the past three years, several different mates had moved in to rent one of the two spare rooms at the house. It was like a revolving door, as one left to continue their journey in life, another was waiting to move in. They couldn't wait to experience life away from their parent's house for the first time. These were all good friends, the majority of which were old school friends who wanted their own independence.

Alan, who I'd known for many years, moved into the box room. He was a member of staff at the local golf range. This came in handy, not just for my golf practice, but the fact they had a great sports bar on site too, where we would spend a lot of time drinking the night away. Alan was a small, skinny, unkempt lad with long, dark blonde, swept-back hair and a bushy ginger beard. He was only two years older than me, but we always joked that he looked a lot older.

Brunden was happy in the room overlooking the rear garden. As with Paul before him, he was a bit of an IT wizard and was more than happy that Paul had left his computer desk behind. Brunden was quite the intellect in the group as we grew up together through school. He was always destined for bigger things. He stood around six feet tall, very gangly, with a bit of a pot belly and had spiky, gelled, mousey hair. He was the skinniest fat kid I knew.

As I spent the majority of my weekends at work, I had the choice of which day to have off in the week, and I opted for Fridays. Fridays worked well, as my now retired dad would take me golfing to Beauchief golf club. After our round of golf he'd take my golf clubs home with him. I would then walk down to the Beauchief hotel to meet a few of the lads for the evening festivities ahead.

The Beauchief hotel was a grand, stately-looking building with two bars and a restaurant which had been renovated in keeping with modern times. Every Friday they would hold a Motown night. The DJ was brilliant, playing all the classics and getting everyone up for a dance. In the summer the gardens were stunning and hundreds of people would come to dance and drink until the doors closed around two in the morning.

What I didn't know is that my future wife was the events and bar manager there. She would often see me walk in on a Friday evening. Unbeknown to me I was known by all the staff there as the orange T-shirt guy. I did wear some pretty lairy clothes whilst out golfing and I'm not the kind of guy to care what anyone thinks about how I dress, so I'd go straight to the bar dressed in what I had been wearing that day.

On one particular Friday night, I went to the upstairs bar for a drink and a male member of staff behind the bar pushed this gorgeous-looking, petite brunette towards me to take my order. It was the first time we'd spoken, and I stared at her long, flowing dark hair, olive skin and large blue eyes, as she asked me, 'What can I get for you?' I ordered the round of drinks for myself and three of my friends and ended up having a bit of a chat afterwards. Grace was not only very pretty, but seemed like a really nice lass too, so we hit it off from the get-go.

Over the coming weeks, Grace and I enjoyed our first few dates, when my brother Darren told me that a new casino had opened in town. He'd heard of their award-winning chef before and the food did look delicious judging by the menu he'd sent me. The following Saturday we decided to book and go for a double date. Darren, his wife Lisa and Grace would be joining me.

Grace arrived at my house in the early afternoon that Saturday to get changed before the big night. She was looking forward to meeting my brother and his partner Lisa for the first time. Brunden and Alan had agreed to vacate the house for the evening and would be stopping at their respective parent's houses.

I, as usual, left it until the last minute to get changed before Darren and Lisa pulled up in a taxi outside. We had a cracking night. The casino was a breath of fresh air and the food was fantastic. We'd all enjoyed our fill of fancy cocktails before we decided to call it a night and ordered a taxi to take us home.

Grace and I were dropped off first as my house was closer to the casino. It was fairly dark as the taxi turned on to my road, apart from the glow of the odd street lamp. The taxi pulled up right outside my home and as Grace stepped out she looked up at the bay window and said, 'Who's the lady in your house? I thought everyone was out for the evening.'
I had one hand in my wallet trying to give some money towards the taxi fare when I stopped what I was doing and alarmingly said, 'What do you mean?'

Grace looked again. I was still sitting in the back of the black cab at this point trying to see what she could see through the steamed windows. I couldn't see anything.

'Who is the old lady in your bedroom window?' Grace pointed as she queried what she could see. At this point I'd stepped out of the cab and was squinting my eyes up towards the large bay window. Again, I saw nothing. I turned to my brother and pulled a face as if to say, don't say anything. I'd not told Grace anything about the hauntings we'd seen or heard. I didn't want to scare her, or worse freak her out from coming round to my place.

As we got to the bottom of the path, Grace told me the old lady had now gone but was still asking who it was. I said in a reassuring voice, 'There isn't a lady in my house, however, what would you say this so-called old lady looked like?'
Grace, as confident as ever said, 'She looked quite old, with a short grey perm, a cardigan on and her arms were stretched out leaning on the windowsill. She was looking directly at us getting out of the taxi.'

I gulped as I turned the key in the front door after walking up the steep path. I'd heard this before from Craig the week before I moved in. It was pretty much the same sighting. Greg had also seen a similar looking old lady in the front room. But why again could I not see her. Surely this was no coincidence.

Grace and I have spoken about this chance sighting on several occasions. She is still as adamant as ever about what she saw that night and I believe her. After all, she's not the first, and certainly won't be the last to see Mrs. Tompkins.

CHAPTER 10

My girlfriend Grace had now gone back to her original career as a hair stylist. Due to work commitments, I would usually stay over at her house in Totley, Sheffield for a few days mid-week, and she would stop at mine at the weekend. The property she rented was an old Victorian terraced house and definitely not built for someone of my height. Grace would often make fun of me having to walk around the house like the 'Hunchback of Notre Dame', as I ducked and weaved my way through the small door frames, passing from room to room. To me it really was like a 'Hobbit' home. Grace shared the two-bed home with her son Elliott who at the time (2012) was seven years old. He looked like a younger version of 'Charlie', from Roald Dahl's 'Charlie and the Chocolate Factory'. Elliott had the larger room on the second floor, while Grace and I would sleep in the attic room, another room I struggled with for head clearance.

During the early days of our relationship my house mates, Brunden and Alan, would often let me have the house to myself for one night over the weekend, so I could spend some quality time with Grace. Neither of them minded too much about the situation as Brunden had also found himself a girlfriend, and Alan would often stop behind after work until the early hours for a drink, then walk home to his mum and dad's which was just around the corner from the bar where he worked.

Grace worked until 7pm on a Friday night and would drive straight over to mine in her beat-up old Nissan Micra. This worked perfectly, as Elliott's dad would pick him up from school on a Friday to look after him every weekend, at his home in Worksop.

Grace would always arrive home to see me waiting at the front door with a glass of wine in my hand for her and the house spotlessly clean, with scented candles burning throughout the front room and kitchen. You'd think this was me trying to be romantic and I suppose it was in a way, but the main reason was the house was a real lad pad during the week. Three lads, with mates coming over all the time for a drink. It was never going to be tidy during this time, and the smell throughout wasn't the best either.

The main reason for the bad smell was poker night, which was hosted by me once a week on a Thursday. Twelve of us would battle it out to see who the champion would be. We had two tables set up, one in the front room and one in the kitchen. We'd play until three people from each table were left and then place the remaining six people at the kitchen table, where we'd all gather to watch the champion rake in their winnings.

I loved the poker nights or 'lads' night' as everyone called it. It was a genuine getaway for all the lads for one evening a week, where we'd get to catch up and share a beer or three. The only issue was that everyone smoked. I never smoked in the house but would let the players in the kitchen smoke if they opened the windows. As you can imagine, this didn't smell too good on a Friday. In fact it got that bad, I had to hire a cleaner to come in once a week on a Friday to make sure the house was spotless for Grace's arrival.

I wasn't the best cook, far from it. I would usually order a takeaway as Grace worked late on a Friday night, and this Friday was no exception. Being a single guy in a house for so long, most of the local takeaways knew me on first name terms and even knew what my order was going to be. Grace however, studied the menu in great detail before telling me what she wanted. After a patient wait, I finally got round to ordering the food.

The local pizza takeaway delivered the food piping hot and in good time. We ate as we watched a film together and shared a bottle of wine or two. Grace usually made me pick the film, but I wasn't allowed to select any horror films. This was a rule set in stone by her. I'm not sure if this was because she now knew of the stories from years in the house, but I adhered to her rule anyway.

After the film we'd always retire to the master bedroom. As you walked into the bedroom you were faced by a large, dark, wooden wardrobe with mirrored panels which spanned pretty much all of the wall to the right. This left just enough room for the king-size bed. The head of the bed lay straight ahead from the entrance and the large bay window where Mrs. Tompkins had now been seen twice was on the left. The room had been carpeted throughout but the cream carpet was now looking a bit tired. The old feature picture rail, three quarters of the way up the walls circled the room.

I've mentioned that we would regularly hear noises throughout the house and this night was no different. I'd drifted off into a deep sleep when Grace shook me awake with a panic in her voice, 'Will, I think there's somebody downstairs, it sounds like there's more than one person too!'

I knew Alan and Brunden weren't due back that evening and as it wasn't too late, I texted them both from my phone to ask of their whereabouts. Sure enough, Brunden was at his girlfriend's and Alan was still at the bar he worked at having a nightcap.

The noises were loud as I peeked round the bay window and looked to the right to see if my neighbour's car was on the drive, signifying that she was home. We never really heard a peep from the adjoining neighbour as these old houses had thick walls. The neighbour was home, but this didn't sound like it was coming from next-door. It was coming from right below us... the living room.

The noise we could hear now sounded like two people in heavy boots pacing from the kitchen into the front room and back again, almost as if they wanted to be heard. I looked at Grace and whispered nervously, 'There's definitely someone in the house.'

Wearing only boxer shorts, I crept to the bedroom door and quietly opened it to the landing. If there was a burglary going on I didn't want to alert them, so I didn't switch the lights on. I gingerly stepped over the creaky floorboard at the top of the stairs and slowly made my way downstairs. As I reached the door to the living room at the bottom of the stairs, the footsteps stopped. The silence was deafening. Gripped with an overwhelming fear I turned the door handle as quietly as I could and anxiously pushed the door ajar, braced ready to punch anybody who had dared to break into my house. The tension at this point was unbearable. My heart was racing out of control. The door was open just enough for me to peek into the room. The curtains were drawn but thin shafts of light pierced through the darkness. My eyes widened as I thrust the door open, fist still clenched.

Suddenly, a loud buzzing noise filled the air.

The big new plasma TV had switched itself on displaying a static screen. It scared the life out of me. I stumbled back in shock into the space at the bottom of the stairs. I could see the static on the screen flashing through the gap in the open door. The noise from the TV was piercing, it echoed throughout the house. More worryingly, I could see the remote for the TV positioned on its stand. The television had just turned itself on.

I let my heart rate settle and gained my composure as I walked through the lounge, fist still clenched. I opened each door to make sure no intruders were in my home. The first door to check was the kitchen, then under the stairs, then through to the utility room. The intensity built more with every door that I opened. I stood in the cold utility room and checked the last door to the downstairs toilet. When I opened it, there was nothing there. Nobody to be seen.

I walked back to the front room and turned the TV off, checked all the windows and doors were locked and went back up to the bedroom. How on earth was I going to explain this to Grace?

I don't know how to explain this one, but it certainly gave me a fright. Hearing noises like we did, anybody in their right mind would think it to be an intruder. In one way, I was glad it wasn't but that still doesn't explain what happened, or

how it happened. I spent the next hour in bed that night typing questions into 'Google' on my laptop, 'Can a plasma TV turn itself on?' I'm no television expert but the simple answer I got was...... 'NO!'

CHAPTER 11

Another year had passed, it was now 2013. Brunden had been offered a huge IT job in Edinburgh, Scotland and after considerable deliberation he decided to take it. He drove up with his girlfriend that he'd met whilst stopping at mine and ended up renting a house in the city centre.

Alan was also on the move, he'd been on the list to get a council house for around seven years, and was finally offered a place in Lowedges, Sheffield.

I was now living alone again for the first time in years. Grace and I had hit a bit of a rough patch too. I'd randomly purchased a hair salon and employed Grace as the manager, as I knew nothing about hair. They do say don't mix business with pleasure and I understand why now. We'd been together two years and the working relationship had taken its toll, so the split was almost inevitable.

I was beginning to realise the hair salon purchase was a mistake. I was still working full time as a manager at the car retailer in Rotherham and ended up spending my one day off a week managing constant issues at the salon. No more golfing on a Friday with my dad.

I'd still see several of the lads a few days a week and we still enjoyed our Thursday poker night, but when everybody left the house of an evening it felt very empty. When I was on my own, most of the time it was quiet. There wasn't much to report on the paranormal front, apart from the odd strange noise or loud footsteps from an invisible presence.

During the evenings I'd very rarely cook and just order in from whichever takeaway took my fancy. To save a little bit of money, as I lived alone, I'd always drink water when I wasn't drinking beer. This does come with its health benefits, but as I said before my body wasn't exactly a temple and after gorging on takeaways every night it was never going to be.

When I poured a glass of water, I'd always use a pint pot and as in most lads' kitchen cabinets, there were plenty to choose from. Most of them were probably taken from local pubs by the many visitors I'd had over the years. To save on the washing up, I'd take a glass from the cupboard as I walked in from work, fill it with water and reuse the same glass that evening. Sometimes I'd even use it the next morning too before placing it in the sink ready to wash the following evening.

On one particular night, I followed this same ritual

and filled my pint glass with water. I'd ordered food from the local Indian takeaway and sat myself down in the front room, with my feet up, ready to watch the TV all night.

I'm not a messy person and always kept the house clean and tidy, washing pots, wiping down kitchen sides and usually whipping round with the hoover at night.

I used that same glass all night and as with every other night, I placed it on the kitchen side ready for reusing in the morning before going to work. I went to bed, awoke around 7am and went downstairs into the kitchen. I looked to where I'd left the glass and froze in terror. In its place was a neat pile of glass fragments. How the hell had this happened? How could it even be possible? I asked myself.

It wasn't just the fact it was smashed into smithereens, it looked like it had then been carefully brushed together to form a perfect little pile in the centre of the kitchen worktop. I couldn't believe my eyes, a cold shiver ran down my spine. Firstly, I don't understand how it could break on its own and secondly, there wasn't really any mess. There wasn't a single shard of glass on the floor.

I'd never seen this happen before and this strange occurrence marked the beginning of an unsettling series of poltergeist activity at

number 333.

CHAPTER 12

Later in the year of 2013 I had a chance meeting with a girl named Sadie. Sadie was a small, average build, 25-year-old lass from the other side of Sheffield. She had short, dyed red hair in a bob and a freckly complexion.

We first met when I broke the golden rule of Thursday lads' night. Girls are not allowed, that was pretty much the only rule of lads' night, and me being the founder of the whole thing had broken that rule.

Lara, who was a dear family friend of mine whom I'd known pretty much all her life, had been pestering me for a long time to come and play poker at my house. She'd heard on the grapevine, through her brother Riley, who played every Thursday, that we had a good thing going, and really wanted to get in on the action. I consulted the lads one Thursday and they agreed that she was pretty much like a sister figure to me, and we should let her play.

When I broke the news to Lara, she was ecstatic and immediately started taunting me that she was going to win and take all our money. I saw Lara as one of the lads, she had a very boisterous demeanour, scraped back light brown shoulder length hair and every-time I saw her she seemed to have a cigarette in one hand and a can of cider in the other, a real character.

She told me about a friend of hers from work who was looking for a place to live and knew I had two spare rooms I could potentially rent out to her. I'd never had any females living with me, apart from my fiancée and that hadn't lasted long. Other than that, pretty much every mate I'd ever known had had a stint at number 333.

The house did still feel a little empty, so I asked Lara if she could bring her friend Sadie along to lads' night and introduce her to everyone including me.

Sadie and I got on like a house on fire. During the evening we agreed terms and I was excited to see her move in the following day. As all the lads were sitting around playing poker during the discussions, they said it would be a great idea to have a housewarming party on the Saturday, to welcome Sadie properly. They didn't have to force my arm because I loved a house party.

Sadie moved into the larger of the spare rooms at the back of the house and soon adorned it with her things. I'd never seen the room with a feminine touch before, but I must admit it did look a damn sight better than any previous housemate's attempts. She did go a little over the top with the fairy lights though.

As Saturday came around, we did a big shop to get all the alcohol and barbecue food we would need to feed the masses for the housewarming. My friends started to arrive around 6pm and luckily the weather had been kind to us. The garden and house were soon buzzing with people. The beer was flowing, loud music playing, and everyone seemed to be in good spirits. We were having a great evening and it was good for Sadie to meet all my friends.

The party went on to the very early hours and the last few stragglers were busy ordering taxis as people drifted away into the night. Soon there was just the three of us, Sadie, Seth and I were the last ones left. Seth was a friend of a friend really, we didn't know each other that well but mixed in the same circles. He was quite a small, chubby lad in his late 20's with greying, short, swept-over hair and he'd always be wearing the latest designer cloths. He seemed a nice lad.

Seth had tried to order a taxi but was having no luck, while Sadie and I tidied up the place as best we could. Seth then asked politely if he could stay on the sofa and order a taxi to leave first thing in the morning, as he had work in the afternoon. I was so tired and ready for bed myself that I agreed. I would usually offer up the box room, but it was currently full of my washed clothes, waiting to be hung up.

Sadie and I wished Seth a good night and headed up to our separate rooms. As I left the front room I turned and told Seth that the keys were in the back of the door should he want to leave early in the morning. I told him not to disturb me when he left, then I turned off all the lights and headed upstairs.

I heard Seth leave at around 9am that morning. I'm not sure if it was the noise of the black cab outside or him slamming the front door shut, but he'd definitely gone. My hangover had well and truly kicked in at this point, so I wasn't going to get up to see him off.

I must have fallen back to sleep but woke up again around 11am with a stinking headache. There was a lady renting a room in the house now, so I had to get partially dressed before making the long walk downstairs to get a glass of water. I couldn't just walk around in my boxer shorts anymore.

When I got to the top of the stairs, I noticed the front door had been left ajar, not fully open, but it certainly wasn't closed. I ran downstairs fearing the worst. Had an opportunist seen that the house had been left unlocked and helped themselves? I quickly opened the door to see if my car was still there. It was. However, Sadie's handbag was on the path outside with its contents strewn all over the place. I ran upstairs to get Sadie and told her to come and look to see if anything was missing.

In a panic, Sadie ran down the stairs and I helped her pick up the items outside the front door. All her belongings which included a phone, a purse, a packet of cigarettes and lots of differing make-up were still there. As Sadie picked up the contents of her bag, she looked at me and said, 'I can't believe this has happened. The weird thing is whoever did it hasn't taken anything. All my stuff is still here.' I apologised. This was my fault; I could have locked the door as Seth left but I'd decided not to at the time.

We both walked back into the living room through the door at the bottom of the stairs, breathing a sigh of relief. Secretly, I was dreading to see if my TV or any other belongings had gone.

It was much worse than that. As we walked into the front room our eyes were drawn immediately to the sight of five very sharp, large knives stuck into the wooden floorboards blocking the threshold to the doorway of the kitchen. These knives ranged from four to eight inches long and each one was a good two inches deep into the floorboards. I recognised the knives straight away; they were usually housed in a knife block in the kitchen. They were also spaced equally apart, in size order across the foot of the doorway. We looked at each other in disbelief before I asked Sadie to remain in the front room while I apprehensively investigated the rest of the rooms downstairs.

I stepped over the knives and entered the kitchen. Two cupboard doors and one of the drawers where the cutlery was kept were all wide open. The knife block was empty on the kitchen worktop. Nothing else was missing.

I phoned Seth and caught him before he'd started work. I was extremely stressed out by the whole situation, and I think he could tell this by the frantic tone of my voice. 'Did you do this before you left?' I demanded. Seth gingerly replied, 'Honestly, I don't know what you're talking about. I left the house around 9am and shut the door behind me.' I was shaken up, but I believed him. Thinking about it, I remembered hearing him slam the door.

Not a lot of things freak me out about living at number 333, but this particular incident certainly did. Was it paranormal or did somebody sneak into my house while I was asleep? Anybody could have walked in if they'd wanted to; I'd left the door unlocked. But who in their right mind would enter someone's house on a Sunday morning to do such a thing and not take anything from the property? It didn't make sense to me at all. Paranormal or not, it was going to be

a long time before I could sleep easy again. The image of the knives in the floor wasn't going to leave me for some time. The sceptic in me still says there is a logical explanation.

Some friends and family say it's the spirit of the house and the fact it might not like females living in its home. You decide?

CHAPTER 13

Sadie lived with me for around six months, and we shared many a laugh together in the house.

However, early in 2014 I came home from work one night and found that she had left, strangely leaving all her property behind. I informed her family and returned her belongings. It left a sour taste with me as she was behind on her rent and I'd helped in her time of need by providing a room. But as they say... you live and learn.

Once again, I was alone in the house. I put the word out again to the lads to see if anyone would like to move in, not only to help with the bills but to keep me company.

Timmy was the first to respond. We knew of each other at school but didn't kindle our friendship until post school days. We'd often see each other on nights out before he became a regular visitor to number 333, especially on lads' night.

Timmy was a short, stocky lad with a very round shaved head. He worked as a bricklayer and we always ridiculed him because he had the smallest hands for a 28-year-old man that we'd ever seen. Timmy was covered in tattoos; it was like a hobby for him to have something new every few months.

The larger spare room was always everyone's first choice over the boxroom and Timmy was no exception. He took little time in taking down all the fairy lights before moving his own things into the room and personalising it to his liking.

As Timmy had been a friend for a good ten years now, he knew of all the paranormal stories which had happened in the house. However, he was a bit of a lad's lad and didn't believe a word of it. He would always criticise or make fun of anybody who believed in anything of these sorts. Timmy had never been in the house when any of the previous events had happened, so he had no reason to believe in anyone's hearsay.

My brother Darren did quite well for himself as a natural stone specialist, often supplying hotels and residential houses with their new kitchen work surfaces. He'd spent his money buying and renovating houses which he then rented out. Unfortunately, he was having trouble at home with his other half which usually led to him crashing at my house. This was his safe haven except for all the paranormal activity.

Darren arrived one Sunday after spending the day in the pub, only this time he didn't leave. He pretty much set up camp in my spare boxroom. I didn't mind, he was my brother after all and my door would always be open for him if needed.

Darren, Timmy and I got on well and laughter and good times soon returned to the house. Darren would often tell stories to Timmy of the footsteps and the shadow that he'd seen. Timmy was still having none of it, until one day...

Timmy had been at home alone as he arrived back early from work. He was busting to go to the bathroom and hastily made his way up the steep path, through the front door and straight up the stairs into the bathroom.

The bathroom itself was quite unusual. It was fully tiled with large black tiles halfway up the walls finished with white tiles up to the ceiling. The bathroom suite was all black, the toilet straight ahead as you walked in with the sink alongside. The bath ran the length of the room to the right.

Timmy was sweating as he pulled down his trousers and spun on to the throne, just in the nick of time. As he sat there, he stared straight forward at the door ahead. A long string-pull light switch with a metal pendant hung from the ceiling to the right of the door. The pendant was tied to the wall with a small hoop to keep it in place and away from catching in the door.

Timmy's eyes were drawn to the pendant as it hung motionless against the wall in the corner. Suddenly it swung out from the wall about three to four inches and spun on the end of the string right in front of him. It then crashed back against the tiled wall with a bang. Timmy had finally seen something he couldn't explain. He quickly finished his business before making a swift exit; heading downstairs as fast as his legs could carry him.

This story made me laugh at the time as Timmy couldn't wait to tell my brother and me when we got home. It had genuinely scared him, and he said he would probably be using the downstairs toilet for the foreseeable future.

I did however go upstairs to check the logistics of what had happened. As Timmy said, it was impossible for the heavy pendant to lift itself on a string and spin uncontrollably. I tried all sorts of positions with the pendant in hand but failed to recreate the scenario.

CHAPTER 14

A few weeks had passed since Timmy's ordeal with the light switch in the toilet.

It had been a long week at work and the weekend couldn't arrive quickly enough for me. It was going to be my first relaxing weekend I'd had for a long time. The poker night was still going ahead for Thursday lads' night, but I'd decided I wasn't going to go out or have a drink all weekend.

Timmy's son, Hayden was now nine years old. He spent most of his time with his mum, whom Timmy was separated from, and his weekends were spent with his dad. This particular weekend Timmy mentioned to me that he would be stopping at his own mum and dad's as they wanted to see Hayden too.

My brother Darren who was still crashing in the boxroom had weekend plans too. His plans were to stop at my house after a day out at the horse racing on Saturday and he said he wouldn't be back until the early hours of Sunday morning.

That meant both the lads were going to be out on Saturday, so I made plans to catch up on my favourite TV box set, 'Prison Break'. It was going to be a nice, lazy Saturday night. I ordered a takeaway and tucked into a kebab with my feet up and eyes fixated on how 'Michael Schofield' would get out of his next predicament in jail.

I fell asleep on the sofa with a full belly and awoke around midnight before dragging myself upstairs to bed. I didn't hear Darren get home in the early hours, but his night was about to take a turn for the worse...

Darren arrived back at the house in the early hours of Sunday morning, his senses dulled by the amount of alcohol coursing through his veins. His drunken mind was fixed on one thing; more beer. He stumbled into the kitchen, cracking open a can and heading over to the dart board for some half-hearted attempts at hitting a bullseye. As he reached for his can, something caught his eye outside the window. A bright white shape, moving in the shadows of the garden. Darren's heart began to pound in his chest as he stared, trying to make out what it was. Could it be an intruder? The figure moved closer; Darren's fear turned into pure terror. It was a ghostly apparition in the form of an elderly lady floating towards the window with an other-worldly grace. Darren knew of the previous sightings of her but had never experienced it for himself. It matched the description of Mrs. Tompkins.

Darren's hands began to shake as he backed away

from the window. He could only see the top half of the figure as it drifted across from the right-hand side of the window. Darren was now frozen with fear as the ghostly figure suddenly stopped, turned, and looked him in the eyes, before turning its head back to the right and vanishing through the rear of the next-door neighbour's house. Darren clambered into the corner of the kitchen where he sat scrunched in a ball afraid to shout for help.

It was now gone four in the morning and my older brother was calling my mobile phone as I lay asleep in bed. I rolled over to reach the phone which was on the floor next to the bed. I wasn't very happy being woken up at that time when I had to get up for work in a few hours.
'What's up?' I answered in anger.

Darren shakily said, 'Come down here quick!'
I sighed as I put the phone down, stumbled out of bed and pulled my dressing gown on before trudging downstairs. I went through the living room and into the kitchen and saw my big brother sitting, scrunched like a child in the left-hand corner of the kitchen looking absolutely terrified.

I was angry as I walked in the room, but I'd never seen him like this. 'Are you ok, what's happened?' I asked. Darren couldn't get his words out fast enough. He recounted his experience in vivid detail, describing the old lady exactly as others had before, only this time she was translucent; he could see straight through her. She had the same short, grey permed hair, dark cardigan, white blouse and a piercing stare.

My brother was genuinely petrified and was almost ranting now, 'I can't believe I've seen her; she walked straight through the wall into the neighbour's extension!'

I sat with my brother for around an hour before he finally got up off the floor. He continued to stare up at the window. I think he was dreading seeing Mrs. Tompkins again.

My elder brother Darren, who was feared by many had seen a ghost for the first time. He doesn't show his emotions, so to see him like this was a real shock to me. The detailed description he gave me on that night was harrowing to say the least.

In a way I was jealous. If it was Mrs. Tompkins why hadn't she shown herself to me?

CHAPTER 15

The house was like a paranormal hotspot at this time. My brother's terrifying experience dispelled any doubts in my mind that the house was being haunted by an old lady. The assumption was that it was the spirit of Mrs. Tompkins, the first owner of the house.

I was beginning to see quite a lot of a good friend of mine, Ian. He'd come round most Thursdays and usually visit on a Friday and Saturday too. We'd known each other a few years from the same circle of friends and he'd recently been round to fix my boiler, as he worked as a gas engineer. Ian was really into his football, like me, and we are both avid Sheffield United supporters. When he came round to fix the boiler we ended up watching the game and having a few beers. This had become a regular weekend thing for the both of us and Darren would often join us for a drink too.

Ian was a tall guy and always had a fresh haircut; shaved short on the sides with messy light-coloured hair on top. He always dressed well and prided himself on his appearance. He also had a distinctive lazy eye which he would constantly ridicule himself about. In his words, 'It's like I could have one eye on you and one on the TV.' Ian lived just down the road with his girlfriend, Georgia and four-year-old son, Jack.

Ian's girlfriend wore the trousers in their relationship, and he'd usually have to tell a little white lie if he wanted to get out for a drink with the lads. One Saturday, he came round to watch the late kick off football match at 5.30pm and didn't leave until gone 11.30pm. He'd told his partner Georgia that the match went to extra time, then penalties and each player had to take five penalties each in their squad. Most people know that's not the case, however Georgia was oblivious to this as she wasn't a football fan at all.

The following week Ian asked me to phone him to tell him the boiler had broken down again. Knowing full well that Georgia was within earshot he said in a concerned voice, 'Alright, I'll be round soon. I'll bring my tool kit.' All this pretence just so he could come round for a drink.

Grace was back on the scene with me now. We'd been apart a year and had clearly missed each other, so we started dating again. She was also round at mine on this particular Saturday and got on well with Darren and Ian. Timmy was at his parents' again with the little one, so the four of us enjoyed an evening of playing darts followed by lounging around watching the TV with a drink in hand.

It was getting late, and Grace mentioned how tired she was, so we both headed off upstairs to bed. Ian had asked if he could stop on the sofa and walk home the following day as it was too late, and he didn't want to wake young Jack. Darren was asleep in the armchair in the front room, and I gave the nod of approval for Ian to camp down on the sofa for the evening.

It was a warm evening, so Grace opened the bedroom windows before we got into bed. With the windows open you would hear the odd car go down the road but at this time of night they were scarce in numbers.

As I was just nodding off to sleep, I heard what sounded like two or three people walking up the steep path to the front of the house. I knew it was my path as I heard them step on the metal grate at the top of the path, just before the front door. As the heavy-footed trespassers reached the front door, one of them said in a whispered voice, 'Let's go round the back.'

I jumped up out of bed, wondering what the hell was going on. Grace awoke startled, looked at me and said, 'Who was that?' I looked out of the bay window but didn't see anybody. I quickly ran into Timmy's room to look through the window onto the back garden, but again there was nobody to be seen.

I leapt downstairs as fast as I could to check things out. Ian was sitting with a blanket pulled up to his eyes, looking very nervous. 'Who was that?' he asked in a panic. He'd heard the same footsteps and the whisper. Darren was still fast asleep in the armchair and oblivious to the disturbance. The weird thing was, we'd both heard the footsteps stop as they got to the front door and then nothing. Like they'd just vanished.

I'd heard things like this before but for three of us to hear the same thing was really strange. This was now the second time that something had happened outside the house in the past two weeks. Things were certainly hotting up at number 333.

Ian didn't close his eyes that night after I left to go back upstairs to Grace. He looked completely drained and concerned when I saw him the next morning. We debated what or who it could have been. It does seem that there's a more rational explanation to this event, some lads up to no good maybe. However, why did the footsteps suddenly stop and why couldn't I see anyone through the windows? How could they disappear without a sound?
Another incident that left me wondering... is it paranormal or not?

CHAPTER 16

Over the past six months a lot of strange things had been happening at number 333, but it had been quiet for the past month, until now...

Another good friend of mine from my school days, Bob, was a regular visitor to the house most weekends. I'd very rarely see him during the week as he worked as a site manager for a large construction company and would often be working away in different cities.

We'd not really met until our later years in education at the age of around fourteen. He was average height with jet black spiky hair and always clean-shaven. He was a really nice lad to be around and enjoyed a good laugh.

One particular Saturday I arrived home from work to find Darren, Timmy and Bob listening to the football results on TV. Bob called himself a Sheffield Wednesday fan but wasn't really into football at all, so he just sat quietly sipping his drink. As I was a staunch Sheffield United fan, Bob was lucky to be allowed in my house in the first place.

It had been a long day at work, and I was ready

for a drink myself, so I quickly greeted the guys in the front room before making my way into the kitchen. Bob shouted, 'There's vodka in the fridge, get one down ya!' I poured a vodka and coke and joined the conversation as we discussed the events of the day.

This Saturday seemed like a fairly normal start to the weekend. The lads were in good spirits and we'd taken to the kitchen to enjoy a game of darts. I never quite understood this, but I was always ridiculed for winning at darts no matter what format we played.

It was getting late and I'd had quite a bit to drink, so I said goodnight to the gents and retired to bed. Timmy and Darren also retired to their rooms. Bob had asked if he could stay on the sofa and leave in the morning, which as always was fine with me.

Before he retired to the sofa, he said he was going to have a cigarette in the back garden and I reminded him to make sure to lock the back door after he'd finished.

Bob finished his smoke and made his way back to the front room. He shut the door at the bottom of the stairs and closed the door to the kitchen before switching the light off. His bed for the night was the three-seater leather sofa and Bob settled down under the warm throw. I'd installed black-out curtains in the front room, so the room was now pitch black. It was shortly after, just as he was drifting off to sleep, that things started to get weird. Bob was not going to get much rest that night...

Suddenly the door to the kitchen started to creak open. Bob peered through the darkness towards the shaft of light entering the room. He nervously got up from the sofa and walked through the door into the kitchen. The only rational explanation he could think of was that he'd left the back door open when he'd been out for a cigarette. He checked the door; it was closed and locked. All the windows were shut too. He slowly went back through the kitchen door and sat down on the sofa.

He was fully alert now and his mind was working overtime. How on earth had the door opened when there was no draught? Just as he was trying to get his head around what had just happened the TV suddenly burst into life. It had turned itself on, emitting a loud buzzing noise. Static flashed across a brown screen as Bob's heart began to race. He was frozen with fear. He quickly checked to see if he'd accidentally sat on the TV remote but panicked even more when he saw it resting on the armchair.

Before he had time to think, the TV suddenly switched itself off and the room was deathly quiet again. The door to the kitchen then slowly began to move again, creaking shut with an eerie sound that shook Bob to his core. There was an electric atmosphere in the room as Bob thought about shouting upstairs for help. He was too petrified to do so. He was sure he could feel a presence near him. Bob was not alone, and he knew it.

I remember Bob telling me all about his story the following morning. I came downstairs to find him sitting, wide awake on the sofa with the light on. He'd not slept a wink. The panic was still in his voice as he tried to explain what had happened.

Bob now lives in Cheshire with his girlfriend Kelly. I phoned him to get all the details correct for this story and he told me how the events unfolded in great detail. His voice was still shaky even after all this time. The memories of the night he spent on my sofa stay with him to this day and will probably never leave him.

CHAPTER 17

It was early 2015, Timmy had decided he wanted his own place and rented a house from his brother at Halfway in Sheffield. Darren was trying to rekindle his marriage with Lisa and had moved back into his family home. Once again, I found myself living alone at number 333.

As my mum and dad had both been retired for a few years now, they would often go on holiday both in the UK and abroad. Whilst they were away they would ask me to look after their beautiful dog, Guinness. Guinness was a female, medium-sized, short-haired black and white Border Collie, or sheep dog as the breed are more commonly referred to.

Guinness had been my brother's dog since being a young pup and as she grew older, he realised she would need walking regularly and felt he didn't have the time. My dad jumped at the opportunity to adopt her as his own. My dad had grown up with a Border Collie as his family dog when he was a young lad, so he loved it when Darren visited with Guinness. My dad loved walking and playing ball with the dog and had time on his hands, so it was a perfect match.

My mum and dad informed me they were going away for a week to Fuerteventura and asked if I would look after her. I was more than happy to do this, and they dropped Guinness with me one Wednesday evening, with her bed, lead and enough food and treats to see her through the week.

I'd never met a dog as clever as Guinness. She had a human-like facial expression when you spoke to her. She was so obedient and well behaved. She really was one of a kind and would follow you wherever you went. Guinness was so clever you didn't need to walk her on a lead. She'd stop at the edge of pavements and sit and wait until you told her it was ok to cross the road. She was the perfect dog, and everybody loved her.

She had now been with me for a couple of nights. It was Friday night and the two of us were enjoying a lazy night; Guinness sound asleep in her bed and me with my feet up watching TV. The house felt so quiet and peaceful, but after a while I decided to turn in and have an early night. I looked down at Guinness and said, 'I'm a bit tired now, time for bed pal.' She looked up at me and wagged her tail in acknowledgement.

There was a tall lamp in the front room, in the corner next to the three-seater leather sofa. It had a wire frame which was covered in a paper-like, white material with a single bulb inside which softly illuminated the room.

There were no other lights on in the front room as I turned off the TV and walked over to the lamp to switch it off. To do this I had to press a foot pedal that led from the lamp to the wall socket. I hit the pedal, but the light stayed on. I scratched my head and tried again, only to get the same result. The light wasn't going off. I reached behind the sofa, where the lamp was plugged into the wall socket, and hit the switch next to the plug. Still the lamp remained on. I was now baffled so I decided to unplug the lamp from the wall socket. With the plug in my hand, I was now standing, completely bamboozled, as I stared at the glowing lamp in front of me. I took a picture of myself holding the plug and cable and sent it to a friend of mine, Steve, who was an electrician. In the accompanying text I asked him how this could be possible. With a shrug of my shoulders and Guinness's doting eyes staring up at me, I decided to leave it and go to bed.

As I got to the top of the stairs, Guinness took up her usual spot at night, with her front paws over the top step and her head resting on them. She would stay there, looking downstairs before falling asleep, not moving or making a noise all night. Guinness would also do this at my mum and dad's It was almost as if she was protecting you as you slept, by keeping an eye on the front door. I brushed my teeth and clambered into bed alone.

As I lay there, I received a text message from my pal the electrician. It read, 'That's not possible mate, how have you done that?'

Worried, I phoned Steve straight away hoping for some sort of clarity, but deep down I knew there was no logic to it. I explained the situation, step by step and he replied, 'Mate, that is weird... these lamps don't have an internal power source. There is no possible way it can stay on once it's either switched off or unplugged. Something strange is going on.'

We ended the conversation, and I thanked him for getting back to me so quickly. I lay there puzzling over this latest paranormal event. I couldn't rest and laid awake, turning things over in my mind. Was it paranormal? Surely, it must be... there's no logical explanation for it. My mind was working overtime and as nervous as I was, I decided to turn off the bedroom light and try to get some sleep. As I pulled the quilt over my eyes, I was mindful of the fact that when weird things like this took place, they were usually followed by something bigger or stranger soon afterwards.

The story of the lamp that wouldn't switch off is still a mystery. That evening I left it unplugged but it continued to illuminate the room. The cable and attached plug were in the middle of the

floor and nowhere near a power source.

However, things didn't end there, and I was about to experience one of the scariest nights... yet!

CHAPTER 18

That same night Guinness was poised at the top of the stairs in her usual night-time position, laid down with her front paws draped over the top step and her chin tucked tightly between them. She was settled for the night.

Usually at night I would close my bedroom door but tonight, for some reason I'd left it ajar. A narrow beam of light from the streetlamp outside pierced through the window at the top of the stairs, through the gap in the door and across the foot of the bed. Guinness, who would normally be silent was making a shuffling noise. It sounded like the excitable movement she would make when she'd been greeted by somebody or when she was about to be given a treat. Whenever something like this happened, she'd usually lie as she was now, with her head on her front paws and wiggle her hind quarters, wagging her tail uncontrollably. This was what I could hear through the gap in the door. I couldn't see Guinness but the noise was getting louder, and it was pitch black apart from the slither of light cast across the bed.

I was already a bit shaken up by the earlier mystery

of the lamp that wouldn't switch off and decided to shout Guinness to come into the bedroom so she could sleep at the foot of the bed. As I opened my mouth to speak, I heard a chilling man's voice from the staircase whisper strongly... 'Come here!'

I froze. I couldn't move for fear. The hairs on the back of my neck stood up as I lay there petrified. This wasn't paranormal. Someone was in my house; I was sure of it. I somehow composed myself to jump out of bed, looking for something to use as a weapon. I couldn't find anything, so in desperation I slid open the wardrobe door, pulled out all my clothes and grabbed the metal rail that they'd been hanging on. I crept towards the bedroom door, wearing only my boxer shorts, and wielding a hollow metal bar.

Fear gripped every inch of my body as I nervously pushed the door open. I could still hear the noise from Guinness, but I could now see that she was looking at something at the bottom of the stairs, her back-end still wiggling away. I nervously looked over the top of the banister rail into the dimly lit staircase. Guinness was staring at something, but I couldn't see what it was.

I walked over the creaky floorboard at the top of the stairs and stepped over Guinness. I proceeded cautiously downstairs and as I reached the bottom step, turned, and grabbed a seven-iron from my golf bag that was propped against the wall. I put the metal bar down as quietly as I could so as not to disturb the intruder. Before plucking up the courage to open the living room door, I glanced back upstairs. Guinness was still wiggling away. This was really strange as she'd always follow me around the house except for when she guarded the stairs whilst I slept.

I took a deep breath and burst through the door, wielding the seven-iron expecting a confrontation. There was nobody there. I turned on the lights and rushed into the kitchen, checking the door which led under the stairs, with the club held high in the air ready to strike. Nothing... Nobody! I continued into the freezing cold utility room and checked the last room, the downstairs toilet. Again nothing, no intruder.

I walked back through to the front room, still shaking and sat on the sofa, holding the golf club tightly in my hands. Guinness stayed put at the top of the stairs. Whatever was down here with me, she wanted nothing to do with it.

I eventually went to bed that evening, walking past Guinness as she guarded the stairs. This time I closed the bedroom door.

Not many things have scared me in my house. This however did. Looking back and thinking about the voice that night sends shivers down my spine to this day. Who or what was that?

CHAPTER 19

It was now May of 2015 and although I was now living alone, my relationship with Grace was growing stronger. I was the happiest I'd been at work in a long time. The team I'd built around me at the Rotherham site were a great bunch of lads and lasses and we'd turned a sales team that was losing money year after year into a profitable department.

I arrived at work one morning and went to make myself a cup of tea in the communal kitchen. It was a ritual I normally performed before gearing myself up for the morning sales meeting. In the kitchen I was greeted by the sales director for the division who asked if I would have a chat with him and the Rotherham site boss in the main office overlooking the showroom. I obliged and sat with the two of them for a conversation that caught me off guard.

I was informed that the company was making some internal changes and they wanted me to take a promotion as general sales manager at the Chesterfield site. This particular site was having serious personnel issues and morale was at an all-time low. Senior management had seen what I'd achieved with the team at Rotherham and obviously thought I could replicate it at Chesterfield.

I was flattered but loved working with my team so much, I decided to turn the offer down. I could see from the sales director's face that this wasn't the outcome he'd hoped for, and he left the room looking very perturbed. I thanked him for the opportunity and got on with my team's morning meeting.

A few weeks passed when I was basically told I would have to take the position in Chesterfield. I resented the decision but had to remain professional about it and make the move.

Being a people person, I spent the first week in my new role getting to know the staff and held one to one meetings with them all. I needed to understand what was causing the low self-esteem within the team. I also planned a work night out around Dronfield, the local village near my new workplace, to do a bit of team building. This was to take place the following Saturday.

The night out was a great success and we pub crawled our way through Dronfield into the early hours, until there were only four of us left. The other three were Shane, my workshop foreman, Harry, one of the sales team, and Aidan, the local resident singer from the last pub we'd visited.

As the pubs closed, I invited the three of them back to my place but warned them that my house was haunted. Aiden and Shane were quite intrigued by this, but Harry just laughed and ridiculed me for believing in such rubbish.

Harry was a tall lad and solid as a rock with a very muscular physique. He was a few years younger than me in his mid-twenties and had short, shaved, brown hair. He was the sort of guy that knew how to handle himself and you could see from the small scars on his face that he'd been in a scrap or two in his time.

As we made the fifteen-minute taxi ride back to my house I enlightened them on some of the paranormal activities that had taken place since I'd been in the house. Harry continued to mock me but did say he was looking forward to a beer and a game of darts.

We arrived back at my house and I led them through the living room and into the kitchen, passing each of them a cold beer from the fridge. We set up to play a game of darts and I put some of my favourite music on that I'd downloaded over the years.

It was Harry's turn to throw and as we all stood watching, he stopped for a moment, dart in hand. 'What's that noise?' he queried as he stared at me with a worried look on his face.

I had no idea what he'd heard, so I turned the music volume down to listen in. I was startled to hear the heavy footsteps were back with a vengeance upstairs. It sounded like whoever or whatever was making the noise, was pacing from the largest spare room onto the landing and back again.

Harry confidently said, 'You're winding us up, there's someone upstairs isn't there?' I told him there were only the four of us and nobody else was in the house. Aiden and Shane looked at each other a bit shocked, aware of the stories I'd told them earlier of heavy footsteps often being heard.

Harry put the darts down on the kitchen table before hastily walking out of the kitchen into the living room to try and prove me wrong. As he got to the door at the bottom of the stairs, we all heard a metallic noise; the sort of sound you'd hear if somebody had just hit a musical triangle. Immediately after, the heavy footsteps upstairs stopped. Harry ran back into the kitchen looking shell-shocked saying, 'What the hell!'

The three of us stood staring in disbelief at Harry, awaiting an explanation as to what he'd just seen or heard. Harry was now visibly shaking and tried to speak but the words wouldn't come out. He was almost dumbstruck.

'What's happened?' we all questioned. Harry tried

to compose himself and finally managed to spit the words out. He explained that as he was walking through the front room, the door to the hallway was slightly ajar and he could see a bunch of keys hanging from the lock in the front door. The keys then spun a full 360 degrees right in front of him, and then came to an abrupt stop. This noise explained what the other three of us had heard from the kitchen.

Harry being Harry still didn't believe what was going on. He took a big swig from his can of beer to calm his nerves and after some soul searching, we tried to resume our game of darts. No sooner had the first dart been thrown, the sound of heavy footsteps could be heard once again, pacing across the floor above our heads. I turned the music down again and we all stood in silence as the footsteps continued upstairs.

Harry again hastily made his way out of the kitchen to the foot of the stairs, where he bravely walked up slowly. As he got to the landing at the top of the stairs we heard him stop, just as the other disembodied footsteps had stopped too. A few moments later we heard what sounded like a baby elephant running down the stairs. Harry ran back into the kitchen. 'There's something not right up there, I believe you now!' Harry stammered.

Harry explained that when he'd reached the top of the stairs the heavy footsteps had suddenly stopped, and everything was silent again. He thought the noise had come from the spare room at the back of the house, so he'd opened the door and immediately felt a presence in the room. He said there was a static electricity in the air, the kind that makes the hairs on your arms stand up. He'd frozen for a second before running out of there and back to us as fast as he could.

Harry couldn't wait to tell the team at my new job over the coming days and was now of the same mindset as me. He had witnessed for himself some unexplained phenomena and would not be ridiculing me again anytime soon. He said he now had an open mind about the paranormal activity at number 333.

CHAPTER 20

Christmas 2015 was the first time I'd spent the holiday season with Grace. We were both in the spirit of the season and I'd purchased a real Christmas tree for the first time ever. I really enjoyed this time of year as I'd get to see my family, wear horrendous festive jumpers and generally be merry.

Strangely enough, Grace and I didn't spend all of Christmas Day together as I'd gone to my parents' for a traditional Christmas dinner. It was still early days in our relationship, so Grace spent most of the day cooking dinner for her son Elliott at their home in Totley, Sheffield.

Later that evening Elliot's dad picked him up to take him over to Wakefield to see that side of his family and Grace drove over to see the evening in with me at number 333.

The following day I had plans to go on a pub crawl around Dronfield for a friend of mine's birthday. My friend Donovan's birthday fell on Christmas Eve and the pub crawl was an annual event in which we'd all gather to celebrate. However, it was his son's first Christmas, so he decided to push it back to Boxing Day as he didn't want to be hungover on Christmas Day.

Donovan was an old work colleague and real good friend of mine. He was about ten years older than me but was always the life and soul of the party. As he was such a popular lad, there was always a great turn out for his birthday, and I'd always make an effort to wear the most horrendous Christmas jumper.

This year was no different. I awoke on Boxing Day next to Grace, had a shower and slipped into my festive outfit for the day. This year I'd gone all out and purchased a handmade novelty jumper. It looked like an old royal-blue school jumper with a round neck. The person I'd purchased it from on 'eBay' had stitched a full-size mechanical talking/ singing reindeer head on to the front of it, and to top it off, its antlers also lit up. Grace looked at me with a disapproving face as I pulled the jumper over my head and said, 'You can't go out with that on!' I agreed to disagree and minutes later my dad arrived to pick me up and take me to Dronfield.

Grace had decided to stay at my house for the day and watch Disney films, have a cheese board and ply herself full of red wine whilst I was out. She was a huge Disney fan and would never get bored of watching the many classic films repeatedly.

At around 9.30pm Grace paused the TV and headed for the downstairs toilet. She walked from the front room, through the kitchen towards the door of the utility room. As she opened the door, she glanced through the glass panel in front of her. It was pitch black outside. Suddenly, a glowing white figure materialised in front of her. Her first thought was that it was simply her own reflection. Grace stood, transfixed, as she quickly realised this wasn't a reflection, it was an old lady in a white night dress. The figure stood outside the window on the back garden staring straight at her. She had short permed grey hair and an empty expression on her face. In a panic, Grace reached around the wall to pull the string for the light in the toilet and as she did so, the old lady vanished. Grace sat on the toilet, her heart racing and shivering with fear. She looked down at her dress and realised it was black. How had she not noticed that it wasn't her reflection straight away? The old lady was in white.

Grace stayed in the toilet for a good ten minutes, too frightened to come out in case the figure was still there. She finally summoned up the courage to make a run for it to the front room, closing all the doors behind her until she made it to the settee and pulled the throw over her. She picked up her phone and called me, 'Please come home!' Grace wailed down the phone.

This was now the fifth sighting of Mrs. Tompkins. Grace pleaded with me to come home

but I could hardly hear a word she was saying as I was a bit worse for wear after a heavy night's drinking.

I do however remember telling Grace that the old lady wouldn't hurt her, and that she'd be fine until I got back.

This was Grace's first time being at the house alone. Was Mrs. Tompkins welcoming her or did she want Grace to leave her home?

CHAPTER 21

It was now early spring 2017. Grace and Elliott had moved from Totley and had been living with me for just over a year. Elliott now slept in the room overlooking the back garden, not that you would see the garden from his room as Elliott was now a pre-teen twelve-year-old and had his curtains closed most of the time. His hobby was computer games and his excuse was that he didn't want any reflections on his TV screen.

I'd left my job as general sales manager at the Chesterfield site for a much larger role within the same car manufacturing brand. I now worked direct for them as an area manager, supporting 25 sites in the Northeast. This meant working Monday to Friday, no more weekend working. It meant a hell of a lot of driving and staying away from home, leaving Grace and Elliott to fend for themselves at number 333.

Over the last two years I'd heard and had to investigate many disembodied footsteps around the house but there were no more sightings in this period.

The house was looking tired; it had officially been a lad pad for twelve years before Grace and Elliott had joined me the previous year. The constant parties and neglect to the house over the years had taken its toll.

Grace and I both had savings and we decided it was time to make the house a family home. We laid plans to completely refurbish the house, new wiring throughout, a new boiler, new bathroom suites up and downstairs, new doors throughout, new windows, a new kitchen, new furniture, new carpets, a tiled floor throughout downstairs, fitted wardrobes, the list goes on… it was going to have a complete overhaul.

I was quite lucky to have plenty of friends, or friends of friends who worked in different trades. I'd done many a favour for most of them over the years by helping source their next car, so I was owed a lot of favours in return and I called them in one by one.

The first job was to rewire the whole property. This was a messy job as the electrician, a friend of a friend, Bill, chased holes into the walls throughout the house. The dust and mess was unbearable, so much so that Grace and Elliott moved into Grace's mum's house, leaving me alone again in the house.

All the furniture and beds had been removed from the house and only the three-seater leather sofa and TV were left in the front room. I used the sofa as a makeshift bed whilst the renovations continued. The day the electrician finished, the painter/decorator and plasterer arrived to crack on with the next jobs on the list. The plasterer, Jason, a tall muscular-built, bald-headed man in his 40's, was filling all the holes in the master bedroom, whilst the painter/decorator, Henry made a start on sanding down the original feature stair banister. Henry was a small, podgy chap in his 60's with grey thinning, mid-length hair and as he worked, he often wore a T-shirt that wasn't quite long enough. You could see his stomach hanging over his trousers at the front, a lovely and professional man all the same.

As Jason was working that evening in the master bedroom it was getting dark. The electrician had removed all the old light fittings and left the new wires hanging from the ceiling in the centre of each room, ready for the fancy new chandeliers to be fitted. I found a small bedside lamp which was boxed away with my belongings and handed it to Jason to plug in and provide some light.

The lamp itself was only small and was controlled by touch on three different dimmer settings. The first touch was for the dimmest setting, the second for the medium setting, and a third touch gave the brightest setting. To switch it off required just a single touch at the end of this cycle.

Jason plugged the lamp in and touched it three times to the brightest setting so he could see to fill and sand the holes in the walls as the dusk closed in.

That night I had plans to watch the latest horror movie. Grace wouldn't entertain watching this kind of film with me, so it was a good opportunity to do so. There were no light fittings in any rooms, so I pulled the three-seater leather sofa into the middle of the front room and put the TV against the wall by the door that led to the bottom of the stairs. The light from the TV was the only light in the front room as I made myself comfortable on the dusty sofa, ready for the night ahead.

As I lay there watching what was possibly the best horror film I'd seen for a long time, I noticed something out of the corner of my eye. A dark shadow appeared under the door to the bottom of the stairs, like a large figure was standing behind it. I paused the TV. This had happened before, but it had been a long time since I'd seen it and I was nervous to investigate. Watching a creepy horror film didn't help with the nerves. I cautiously stood up from the sofa and walked towards the door to open it. As I was about to reach for the door handle, I looked down at the gap at the bottom of the door and saw the shadow move quickly towards the direction of the stairs. I slowly turned the handle and pulled the door open. My heart was racing. Who or what was I about to confront? Silence... nothing. There was nobody in the hallway or on the staircase.

I made my way back to the sofa in the front room and turned off the film. I was so scared I couldn't put myself through watching it. That night was a long one with very little sleep. My imagination was running wild and every little sound in the house made it impossible for me to settle; frightened to shut my eyes.

The next morning Henry arrived first. He had his white overalls on as he was going to be painting in the master bedroom. We talked as I walked into the kitchen to make him a cup of tea. Henry asked me if Jason had spoken to me about what had happened yesterday. I shook my head, 'Why what happened?' I asked. Henry told me that Jason had mentioned that the lamp I'd found for him kept switching itself off. Apparently, Jason classed himself as a bit of a sensitive and could feel when spirits were around him. He'd been telling Henry how haunted the house was and that the spirits were turning the lamp on and off while he was trying to work.

As we walked into the front room continuing the conversation, Henry and I sat on the sofa in the centre of the room, and I told him what had happened to me the previous night with the shadow under the door. As I was telling him this, he suddenly pointed to the gap at the bottom of the door next to the TV. 'Like that?' he shouted.

The shadow was back. This time it was moving as if someone had walked through the front door and straight up the stairs. We both sat staring at the bottom of the door. Henry then looked me in the eyes. He had one hand pointing at the door and a cup of tea in the other.

'I think he's right fella, this place is bloody haunted!' he said with his eyebrows raised.

Both Jason and Henry spent weeks working on the house and both experienced hearing the strange footsteps when nobody was around.

Every morning before they started their jobs on the house, I made them a tea, or a coffee and we'd speak about the mysterious hauntings of the house. I say hauntings as Jason had told me it was more than one spirit.

CHAPTER 22

2019 was a busy year for me and my new little family. We now had two small dogs, Chalky the Cavapoo and Darnell the Pomopoo. Both were cracking little characters and added happiness to the family unit. They differed slightly in size, had short black curly coats with small white beards and a white patch on their chests. We had to go with two breeds of dog that wouldn't shed any hair as my stepson Elliott had bad allergies when it came to pet hair.

The renovations were also now complete. The whole house was looking immaculate, and it genuinely felt like I was walking into a posh holiday home every time I crossed the threshold. I did however throw a bit of a spanner in the works as Grace, Elliott and I sat down at the little dining table in the new kitchen for our evening meal. I was about to tuck into my dinner when I looked around the room at the shiny new quartz worktops and it struck me, something wasn't right. Grace stared at the quizzical look on my face and asked, 'What's wrong?'

I knew that we'd just finished two years of pain with the renovation work going on, but deep down the kitchen I was looking at just wasn't big enough. I wanted to be able to host dinners for family and friends and this just wasn't going to cut it. It was too cramped. I immediately told Grace I wanted to rip the wall out at the back of the house and have plans drawn up for a single-story extension. This would of course mean destroying the kitchen we'd just installed and starting afresh.

Grace wasn't keen on the idea, but it had to be done to turn the house into a proper family home. We slept on it and Grace reluctantly agreed. The next morning, I made the relevant calls to architects and got the planning permission I would need to start the next big job.

The extension took another six months to build, but we now had plenty of room in our new dining room/kitchen with four huge bi-folding doors stretching the length of the rear wall overlooking the back garden. The old lean-to utility room had finally gone. As you walked into the kitchen from the front room, you were now met with a large wooden-topped island which housed the kitchen sink and a few kitchen cabinets beneath it. New kitchen cabinets all grey in colour filled the wall down the left-hand side, with a large gas hob installed beneath them. Floor to ceiling cabinets continued into the dining room extension with a large American style fridge freezer built in. It sounds sad, but I'd always wanted one of those. I purchased a large wooden dining table with bench seats to match, which fitted nicely into the newly acquired space. Above this was a beautiful large orangery glass roof, bringing much-needed extra light into the extension. The table doubled as a pool table and I'm not too sure how I managed to talk Grace into it, but it was a great addition to the final refurbishment. We even had a large decking area installed up to the bi-fold doors in the rear garden. The garden was then finished with artificial grass which was perfect for the two pooches to run around on.

Grace and I had also been planning to tie the knot in a 1930's Art Deco style, black-tie wedding in October of 2019. As I said it was a busy year.

Elliott, now being a fully-fledged teenager at the age of fourteen was very rarely seen other than to come downstairs at mealtimes. Grace loved to cook, she was good at it too and would plan our daily home cooked meals. Now we had the room we often invited family round to join us for a slap-up meal.

We didn't see Elliott very much because he was either revising for his exams or playing on his gaming PC. It was usually down to me to shout upstairs for Elliot to join us at mealtimes. I'd walk to the foot of the stairs and yell, 'Elliott! food time!' This would normally be greeted by a grunt before he eventually trotted downstairs to join Grace and me at the table.

One particular evening around 6pm, Elliott walked into the front room as Grace and I were sat on the new large tan leather corner sofa. We were watching the new TV which was now positioned on the wall by the door to the bottom of the stairs. He walked through the door and stood next to the coffee table in the centre of the room looking confused. 'What were you shouting me for?' he asked.

Grace and I looked up at him with puzzled expressions on our faces. I said, 'What are you talking about, we haven't shouted you?' Elliott grunted, turned and walked back up to his bedroom to carry on with his game. Another half an hour had passed before the same thing happened. This time, Elliott stood in the middle of the room looking suitably unimpressed. 'You've just shouted my name again, what's up?' he blurted.

The two of us looked at each other again and explained that we hadn't shouted him, and tea wasn't going to be ready for a good hour or so. He hung his head in disgust and trudged back up the stairs to his room.

Elliott, for a third time came hurtling downstairs, this time looking quite worried. 'Someone is shouting my name from the staircase, and it didn't sound like you this time Will!'

I was getting a bit concerned now, 'You must be hearing things pal, we've definitely not been shouting you and haven't heard anyone else call your name either.' Elliott stood there looking mystified and insisted that somebody had been calling his name from outside his room. He said it sounded like it was coming from the staircase, where I would usually shout him, but it definitely wasn't my voice that he'd heard.

As Elliott was so young, I'd never told him about any of the unexplained paranormal events that had occurred over the years. I simply didn't want to scare him.

I knew I had to shout if he was going to hear me because he would normally have his headset on, often with the volume turned up loud. I would sometimes have to walk upstairs and knock on his door to get his attention.

There were two things that freaked me out a little about this incident. Firstly, the voice calling his name must have been loud for him to hear it, but Grace and I couldn't hear a thing and he said it was coming from the staircase. Secondly, the fact that Elliott had said it wasn't my voice he'd heard but another man's voice calling his name.

At the time I didn't make much of a fuss about this and basically made out that Elliott must

have been hearing things, but under the surface I was quite concerned that the entity might now be targeting Elliott.

CHAPTER 23

As May 2020 arrived the nation had been plunged into isolation to prevent the spread of Covid-19. The pandemic had turned many families' lives upside down, and ours was no different.

Grace and I had now been happily married for six months. The wedding itself was an absolute blast and we'd enjoyed a small mini-moon (honeymoon) to the Lake District. The national lockdowns however were about to test our relationship.

I was used to working Tuesday to Thursday away from home and was now told I'd be working from home for the foreseeable future. This meant setting the box room up as a fully functioning office. I'd ordered a desk and chair and was working from nine to five, five days a week on my laptop in a tiny little room. Grace however had been completely furloughed from work as she was a hairdresser and for obvious reasons her place of work was now closed during the lockdowns. Grace and I were now spending more time together than we ever had before and as much as we were in love, we were also grating a little bit on each other too. Government restrictions meant you were only allowed to leave the house to purchase essentials from the local stores or exercise for one hour outdoors during the pandemic.

We spent most of our evenings doing the same thing as the rest of the nation, namely drinking too much, eating too much, and catching up on the latest box sets on TV. We'd indulge in the odd quiz via Zoom meetings on the iPad with family and friends too. This helped to break up the monotony of being locked in our home all week. I also looked forward to walking the pooches for an hour a day to get some fresh air and much needed exercise.

One evening on the 20th of May, two days after Grace's birthday, I caught something on video which left me feeling intrigued and Grace petrified with fear...

Over the past six months we'd been hearing a dull thudding sound on the ceiling above the living room. It sounded like somebody was banging on the floor with a clenched fist. The noise was coming from the ceiling and the room above was our bedroom, which was fully carpeted with a thick pile carpet. My adjoining neighbour had gone to live with her parents during the pandemic. That ruled out any noise from next-door. There really was no explanation for the noises and they'd come and go at random times. It could be anytime in the day or night but only when we were downstairs. If one of us went upstairs to investigate the thudding sounds would immediately stop.

The noises would come in ones, twos or threes. It was like somebody was trying to get our attention. Some nights they were so loud we'd hear them above the noise of the TV, which was incredible as we'd had a full surround sound system fitted. Grace and I would sometimes sit with the TV turned off spellbound, as we listened intently to the constant knocking noises. I knew from experience that when I went upstairs to investigate, the noises would inevitably stop, and the house would be left in silence again.

I'd phoned my good friend Matt to tell him about the noises. Matt had lived with me at number 333 back in 2009 and previously rented the box room. He was aware of the paranormal goings on, but neither Matt nor I had ever had the experience of hearing these new knocking sounds before.

Matt was very much like me in the fact he was open minded to the paranormal but always sceptical first. I told him that before the pandemic I'd called on two good friends, a plumber, and an electrician, to check if the noises could be explained logically. They both told me that there was no logical explanation and that quite frankly it was very strange.

Matt told me that these banging noises could be a spirit trying to speak or contact us. He said I ought to ask out and video using my camera phone the next time it happened. I joked that Grace would probably not want to live here if we got a response to a question, but Matt insisted that I should try.

On the 20th of May the thudding sounds started again. One, two... one, two, three... they thudded out, coming from the ceiling directly above where Grace and I were sitting on the sofa. I paused the TV and quickly got out my camera phone. Grace sat quietly next to me as I panned the camera phone round to the ceiling. The only thing that was in shot was the large industrial looking chandelier which hung from the ceiling in the centre of the room. The room was suddenly silent. The banging noises hadn't happened for a good two minutes. I mustered some courage, pressed record, and nervously spoke out, 'Are there any spirits with us now, even if you are upstairs... can you knock twice now?'

Immediately two large distinctive thuds on the ceiling reverberated around the house. What or whoever was with us had just blatantly answered me. Grace, in a stupor nervously laughed and yelled out, 'Oh my god, I want to get out of this house now! Oh my god!' I finished recording and apologised to the spirit/entity. I was stunned and in shock. I was literally too afraid to ask any more questions.

The recording I made that night is still saved on my phone. I've listened back to it on many an occasion and it couldn't be more definite in the way the spirit replies to my question. In a way I wish I'd had the nerve to ask more. That way I might have found out whom I was in communication with, but Grace and I were genuinely too afraid to continue.

The thudding or knocking noises still happen occasionally. When it does happen it usually stops as soon as we investigate. There is still no explanation other than the fact that it is paranormal and somebody from the spirit world is taking up residence in our house.

CHAPTER 24

August 2021 saw the nation finally getting out of all its lockdowns and back into a bit of normality. Face masks were compulsory almost everywhere, but you could finally get to see family and friends for the first time in nearly two years.

Elliott couldn't wait to invite his friends round for a sleepover, not only for them to see his new gaming PC, but also because they'd not seen the house in all its glory since the refurbishment.

One morning during breakfast Elliott asked if two of his best friends could stay over on the Friday night. Grace and I agreed it would be a good idea as he'd not seen them properly for a long time, apart from at school. He text messaged them and the date was set.

That week was like any other week, only this Friday Elliott's two friends arrived at the house to join us for dinner. Grace would usually cook a family meal but thought it would be better to let them choose a takeaway that night. The boys chose what they would like from the local pizzeria menu and we ordered their food.

The food arrived and the lads tucked in at the

kitchen table, before promptly racing back to Elliott's room to take turns playing on the gaming PC. Grace and I finished our food shortly after and retired to the front room whilst chatting about the week's events.

It was now late evening around 10pm and we could hear the odd bit of excitement coming from the lads upstairs, playing their computer games. It was dark outside as I shut the curtains in the bay window, grabbed a bottle of wine along with two glasses and settled down with Grace on the sofa. We were both deep in conversation as the TV played to itself in the background. Suddenly we were both aware that the handle on the door in front of us was slowly turning downwards with an eerie creaking sound. Somebody had to be on the other side exerting pressure on the handle for this to happen.

The door creaked opened slowly as Grace and I watched the gap in the door widen expecting Elliott or one of his two friends to enter. The door opened just wide enough for me to tilt my head round whilst still seated on the sofa. I couldn't see anybody there. The spring-loaded door handle was still down, so someone had to have hold of it on the other side.

I said sheepishly, 'Hello...' and as soon as I spoke the door handle snapped back up and the door slammed shut with a bang! I immediately jumped up off the sofa and ran to the door, opening it quickly. There was nobody there. I looked up into the darkness of the stairwell. Again nothing. Nobody could have gone up the stairs that fast. I walked up the stairs, my heartbeat racing and knocked on Elliot's bedroom door.

I entered the room to see Elliot and his two friends sitting quietly playing on their computer game; Elliott with his headset on. There was no way it could have been them.

The realisation of what had just happened hit me hard and made my heart beat even faster. I stood in the doorway to Elliott's room not wanting to freak them out. I tried to compose myself and asked them if they wanted anything to eat or drink. They all shook their heads and politely declined. I walked back downstairs and into the front room. Grace knew from the worried look on my face that something wasn't right.

There had been five sightings of Mrs. Tompkins from four different people, but I was yet to see her. I'd heard things happen in the house and seen the odd shadow under the door leading to the stairs. I'd also witnessed seeing the knives stuck in the floor but didn't see how they got there. This time I'd seen something happen with my own eyes that could not be explained.

As I stood looking baffled at Grace in the front

room that night, I asked her what she'd seen. She described everything exactly as I'd seen it happen.... the spring-loaded door handle had moved in a downwards motion as if someone was about to enter the room.... the door had opened on its own.... the door handle had snapped back up into its resting position and the door had slammed shut on its own. Grace and I had both witnessed the same thing happen and there was no explanation for it.

This latest ordeal made me feel excited as I'd always wanted to see something paranormal. However, it also left me very apprehensive as to what might happen next.

CHAPTER 25

It was May 2022, only a month before a chance discussion led me to write this book. I'd recently damaged my knee. My right knee and I have a bit of a history to say the least. I'd first damaged it in my mid-twenties playing football and had three surgeries on it, the last being a reconstruction of the ACL ligament nine years ago.

Grace and I loved a weekend city break and had recently booked a trip to York with my good pal Ian and his partner Georgia. Slightly intoxicated on our first night I went over on my knee whilst walking back to our weekend cottage. When I awoke the next morning, my right knee was incredibly sore and badly swollen. The pain was unbearable, so I booked in to see the doctor as soon as I could and after numerous scans, I was informed by the professionals that I had done considerable damage to my knee.

Over the past year I had raised over £2800 for local cancer charities by taking part in dog walking challenges. My dear mum had been diagnosed with a stage four rare breast cancer and had been undergoing treatment for the past four years. She is a fighter and had just finished her first ever prescribed dosages of intravenous chemotherapy. She had gone through the chemotherapy without complaint, losing her beautiful long, thick, dark hair in the process. This must have been devastating for her, but she took it in her stride, purchased a couple of wigs, and made light of the whole situation. Always in high spirits. My mum is a legend.

My long dog walking days were now over. An early Saturday discussion sitting in my living room over a beer with Ian and Doug (my former house mate), gave me an opportunity to raise some money for local cancer charities in a different way.

Doug and Ian were always interested in the paranormal goings on at my house and asked what the latest had been, so I told them...

The week before this I was going to bed on what should have been a normal Friday night. When I got to the bedroom Grace was already in bed and as I started to get undressed, I looked down and saw a strange coin in the middle of the bedroom floor. I reached down and picked up the small bronze coin, it was an American one cent piece. I didn't think much of it but looked over at Grace in bed and said, 'How did that get there? It's an American coin and it was in the middle of the floor.' Grace wearily looked up and said, 'I've got no idea.' For some reason I looked at the date on the coin before putting it in the top drawer of my bedside table and climbing into bed. It was dated 2014.

I'd not really thought much about the coin, but a very strange thing happened the following night. Grace had retired to bed earlier whilst I watched a bit of television. About an hour later I retired to bed myself but when I entered the bedroom my eyes were immediately drawn to a small object on the carpet. I bent down to pick it up and realised it was a coin again. It was in the same spot on the floor as the night before, an American one cent piece with the same date, 2014. When I looked in my top drawer there were no other coins. Grace wasn't quite asleep so I asked her if she'd put it there for a joke, but she had no idea how it could have got there. I tried to be rational about it, but it dwelt on my mind for some time before I popped the coin back in the top drawer of my bedside table and eventually nodded off.

The next day, Sunday, Doug had been round doing some work on the new lights I was having fitted outside of the house. After he left and the evening started to draw in, I went to bed around half an hour after Grace. As I hobbled up the stairs, right in the centre of the staircase sat a coin. I knew this coin wasn't there before because I'd hoovered that day. I picked up the coin and sure enough it was a 2014 American one cent piece. I walked into the bedroom, awoke Grace to ask again, 'You must be winding me up now, did you put that on the stairs?' Grace, not happy that I had woken her up again said, 'Give it here. I promise you it's not me who's done it. I'll pop it on my bedside table, away from you.' I watched Grace place the coin on her bedside table, checked in my drawer to make sure it was the same coin and before I went to sleep, I found myself Googling on my phone: 'Why am I finding American coins in my home?'

The results from the Google search were strange to say the least, but the majority were spiritual people who were saying it means someone close to you is coming to visit. This was weird because a good friend of mine, Paul (my old housemate) and his partner were coming over from America for the first time in three years that coming week. Was it a sign? I didn't know but I went to sleep that night thinking about the reappearing one cent American coin.

When I awoke on Monday morning Grace was still asleep. I walked around the bed and grabbed my towel from the radiator in the corner of the bedroom. I made my way quietly to the bathroom across the hallway, hung my towel on the towel rail and clambered into the bath to take a shower. As I stood there in the shower I was still thinking about the coin and why it kept reappearing when... 'slap!' Something hit me on the back of my calf. Whatever it was had been thrown with some force. I looked down and there it was, in the bottom of the bathtub. It was the same 2014 American coin. I don't know why but before I looked down, I knew it was going to be the coin.

I also didn't feel scared, I was more amazed than anything at what had just happened.

I quickly jumped out of the shower, walked back to the bedroom with the towel around my waist and told Grace what had happened. She looked on her bedside table; the coin had gone. How could this have happened we asked each other. I put the coin on the top of my bedside table. It was still wet from being in the shower. I took a photo and said, 'Don't touch it, I want to see if it moves again.'

I was working from home that Monday, Grace had gone to work. At around 10.30am after finishing an online meeting, I had a chance to grab a quick cup of tea. Whilst standing in the kitchen waiting for the kettle to boil, I phoned my dad and told him what had happened. He was fascinated and asked me where the coin was now. I told him and he asked me to go and see if it was still there.

I walked back upstairs into our bedroom and looked down at the mirrored bedside table. There were still a couple of droplets of water around the coin from the shower incident that morning. It didn't look like it had moved, so I picked up the coin whilst still on the phone to my Dad. 'It's still here.' I said, but when I looked in my hand there were now two American one cent coins. One was dated 2014 and one 2012. In the excitement I explained this to my dad. He laughed and said, 'Bloody hell that's weird, if it carries on, you'll be a millionaire!'

After I'd explained all of this over a beer with Ian and Doug in the front room the following Saturday, Doug, looking very concerned, asked, 'When was I working at your place last?' I told him it was the Sunday he was round, the night before the coin had been thrown at me in the shower. He then worriedly said that when he'd got home that Sunday, he'd taken his work trousers off to put them in the wash, emptied the pockets and found a one cent American coin. We now had three coins between us that had randomly appeared. Doug joked that he hoped no spirits had attached themselves to him and followed him home.

Ian then said, 'That's crazy, you should write a book about all the paranormal things that have happened here. I'd read it, some of the stories are just mad!'

That incident was the latest paranormal thing to happen in our lovely family home.

I seriously hope that more paranormal events take place at number 333 as I've enjoyed researching and retelling all the freaky stories from friends and family who have experienced the many goings on at my home.

Maybe one day I'll even see Mrs. Tompkins...

'AWAKENING THE PARANORMAL' HOME INVESTIGATION

I'd been passing the first draft of my book to a few close family and friends to make sure that it read well before I started writing the second draft. The general consensus was that people loved it, but they wanted more. They needed to see what the experts in this field had to say about the hauntings at number 333.

I spoke with a good friend of mine, Riley (who I mentioned in one of the earlier chapters.) I knew he was into paranormal investigations but had no idea of the scale of his involvement. He told me that he worked with a team called 'Awakening the Paranormal' and they visited around three different supposedly haunted locations per week. They have a huge following across social media where they live-stream all their investigations. I knew then that we had to get the team in to find out more and hopefully shed some light into the hauntings of my house.

As this whole book process had been for cancer charities, Dave, the lead of the team agreed to visit my home for free. The investigation was to be for one night and Dave said he would be bringing all his investigative tools plus two more members of the team.

Riley had visited my house many times before and I'd asked him to keep the location and my name a secret until he drove them here on the 2nd of July 2022. I didn't want anything about the house to be disclosed and to be fair to them, neither did they. They like to investigate and tell you what they find.

The 2nd of July had been a warm, sunny day. I'd shipped my dogs down to my mum and dad's for the night and my stepson Elliott was at his dad's. Grace had gone to stop at a friend's place for the night. My adjoining neighbour had also booked the weekend away, so the semi-detached house that tied to mine was empty too. I was alone in the house for the first time in a long while.

Night was closing in and at around 9.30pm I pulled the curtains, closed all the doors and windows before pouring myself a glass of wine. I dimmed the light to the large industrial-looking chandelier in the front room and sat on the sofa facing the door to the bottom of the stairs, where so many paranormal events had taken place over the years. As I placed my wine glass onto the coffee table in the centre of the room, I leant forward and spoke out.

'Tonight's your night. If there are any spirits in this

house please feel free to come forward and make yourself known. The team will be arriving around 10pm to try and communicate with you. If you need any help or want to move something or show yourself, make sure you do it tonight.' After that I took a big swig of my wine and sat in the silence of the dimly lit house awaiting the team's arrival.

At 10.10pm the Ring doorbell announced the arrival of the investigative team. As I opened the front door I was greeted with a handshake from Riley, who then kindly introduced me to Dave and Kevin. The three of them were carrying all kinds of equipment to set up around the house.

We walked into the kitchen where all the equipment was unloaded onto the table as they went about setting up. Dave promptly told me that he didn't want to know any of the history until right at the end of the night after he had investigated. However, he did need to know where any paranormal hotspots were in the house.

As we were already in the kitchen, I pointed to the space in the extension where the old lean-to utility room used to be. I knew that two sightings of Mrs Tompkins had been right in this spot. As Kevin set up the camera tripod, Riley and Dave went about setting up a small device on the table. The device was a small pyramid, black in colour, with two blue lights on the top. It measured movement and would light up should anything pass by it. The blue light would change to green or red depending on which side it had passed. The team had turned the sensitivity down on this to only detect movement within five to ten centimetres, so they could get a controlled response. Next to this they set up a carbon monoxide detector. I'd seen one of these before as many people have them as an alarm for if their boiler malfunctions. It was a small white device with a display that recorded the amount of carbon monoxide in the air and a small wheel around the number on the screen which was coloured green, amber and red. Luckily for us it was currently flashing green indicating a normal amount of this poisonous gas in the air or we would have had to vacate the property. Riley then placed three small clear balls on the extremes of the table. These were called cat balls and flashed red and blue if they were touched or moved in anyway.

As Riley placed the cat balls on the table, Dave continued to set up three devices on the floor where the bathroom door used to open into the utility room. The first was an EMF meter that measured electromagnetic field changes indicated by a number on the small screen of the white device. If the EMF meter was to spike suddenly it would set off a loud alarm and a small red light on the top would flash. The second was an REM pod. This small device looked like a walkie talkie and measured movement or touch and was again set up to a very small detection area. This device also measured hot or cold spots and would light up red for anything warm, or blue for cold, whilst emitting a shrieking alarm. The last of the three devices placed in this area was an Aeroflux. This small device looked like a security light and was currently lit up green. This would change to amber or red and emit a small beep if the air pressure were to change around the device. There were another six Aeroflux devices leading from the kitchen, through the front room and up the stairs. The aim was to capture any footsteps along this route. About halfway up the stairs sat another REM pod for detecting any presence on the stairs.

Before the team started filming and asking out, Dave walked around near the devices to make sure they were all set to a base line, ready and working. He also used a cable and handheld power detector to make sure that there was no interference from any nearby power sources.

Within one minute of the camera going live and just before Dave asked out, the Aeroflux flashed amber and beeped in the kitchen next to the REM pod.

Dave then proceeded to ask...

'Come on spirit, could you please show yourself to me? Would you like to talk to me? Would you like to tell me something? Why do you keep walking around here? What is your fascination with this corner? Could you make a noise for us?'

As soon as he finished asking the final question, the pyramid on the table lit up red and beeped.

He carried on...

'Could you make a better noise for us or set something else off?'

The carbon monoxide detector on the table started to creep up into the amber range.

'Come on, come closer.'

At this stage the carbon monoxide measurements were going off the scale, the pyramid lit up again in red and the REM pod on the floor screeched loudly as if someone was standing right in front of us.

Dave then asked if the spirit needed any more energy. Riley reached into their bag of tricks on the table which immediately set off the three cat balls. He passed Dave a small circular device and as Dave walked into the corner of the room, he explained to me that he was putting a plasma plate on the floor. The intention was that the plate could help spirits gather energy and hopefully set off devices, move things or even manifest. Dave then placed another circular REM pod to detect any more movement near the devices which had already been going off on the floor.

Dave then spoke again...

'Come on spirit, we know you are here and we know that you know that we are here because of the devices you're setting off.'

An Aeroflux, then a second Aeroflux, both of which were positioned in the front room, went off. This gave the impression that someone was walking towards us and then we heard a loud bang come thundering through the ceiling from upstairs, as if a door had been slammed shut. We all heard it and I explained to the team that we often hear banging and knocking noises throughout the house and that I'd had a plumber and an electrician investigate the noises and they'd found no logical explanation.

We then heard what sounded like footsteps upstairs as two of the devices were sounding their alarms. I told the team that I'd set up my laptop with a sound recorder upstairs in the middle of the hallway, so if that was a spirit walking upstairs, we would have caught the noise. The team were unaware my laptop was recording and this was the first time I'd personally attempted to capture any noises via my computer.

Dave laughed as he looked at the carbon monoxide device which was now flashing dark amber. 'If that gets on to red, we are going to need masks!' he scoffed. He then asked again...

'Come on spirit, set off one of these devices and

show us that you're still here.'

Immediately the REM pod with the alarm for temperature change went off as if a cold blast of air had descended upon it.

Kevin then asked if we could hear somebody running about upstairs. I could hear it, but Riley and Dave couldn't. Maybe I was used to the sounds in the house. As we discussed this the Aerofluxes from the bottom of the stairs all the way into the kitchen went off one by one, as if someone had just joined us from the staircase and was now standing in the kitchen doorway.

I asked the team again if they wanted any history of the house. The answer was a resounding 'no'. I left the kitchen to sit in the front room with a video camera. I faced the bottom of the door to the foot of the stairs where the shadowy figure had been seen many times before. I heard the team in the kitchen discussing the fact that the carbon monoxide device had now gone on to red. The team thought this to be impossible. They placed another carbon monoxide device next to the first one and it read as if everything was ok.

When I re-joined the team in the kitchen, all seven differing devices placed around the table went off alarmingly. I asked if this was something they usually came across. Dave replied, 'No, we can go to some supposed haunted places and nothing happens. We've had all the devices go off so far.

There's definitely something here, we just need to find out who or what it is.'

Dave then placed a phone on the table. He explained to the spirit that if they had anything to say they could do it through the 'app' that they had designed on the phone. It was a word bank that had ten thousand words stored on it and allowed spirits to manipulate the words they wanted us to hear. The 'app' would then speak out the word through the Bluetooth speaker system.

Dave grabbed a handheld digital laser thermometer and pointed it into the corner where all the action was happening on the devices. As he raised the device like a gun to test the temperature, a voice came from the word bank placed on the table...

'*Warm*' followed by '*Tonight*'.

He then asked...

'Can you give me a name?'

The device replied...

'*Robinson*'.

I've changed the name of Mrs Tompkins in the book to keep her identity confidential but what I will tell you is that it's a name not too dissimilar to Robinson. I quizzed the team, 'Would the lady be able to see her name within the word bank?' Dave nodded his head in the affirmative. I tried to think of a way of explaining what I was going to say about the lady's name without giving anything away to the team. Before I had time to react the device then said…

'No, I didn't.'

It was almost as if the lady was answering the question in my head before the words even left my mouth. Perhaps she couldn't see her exact name and opted for something similar.

The Bluetooth speaker went off again, this time exclaiming…

'Outdoors!'

I explained to the team that the phone they'd placed on the table would have been outdoors as it was currently in the newly built extension. Dave asked if the spirit could move any of the three cat balls on the table. Nothing moved. The speaker then went off again…

'Toys' then… *'Shelley.'*

Dave asked…

'Would you like me to call you Shelley?'

Three different devices on the floor all started screaming out at the same time as if the spirit of a lady called Shelley wanted to be known.

Dave asked...

'Shelley, could you tell me what relevance you are to this house? Are you the one that is seen here?'

The device responded with...

'Secret.'

Dave asked again...

'What is the secret, are you keeping your reasons to yourself?'

The speaker responded...

'Get out of here!'

Dave continued the conversation...

'Are you not liking what we're doing? Would you just like to go about things your own way?'

Again, the device responded…

'Comedy.'

Once again, two devices went off in that corner. By this point it was like I was watching a full-blown conversation between Dave and the spirit. The Bluetooth speaker spoke again…

'We hear you.'

Two Aerofluxes went off in the kitchen heading into the front room. The word bank suddenly went quiet, as if the spirit had just walked away from the kitchen and didn't want to talk anymore. In the silence, Dave set up another device. It was another 'app' on a different phone which was linked to a Bluetooth speaker again. This was a different 'app' he and the team had built; it was called the 'sound bank'. There were thousands of sounds and syllables built into the device that spirits could try to speak through by putting noises together to make words and sentences.

Dave asked out…

'Are you male or female?'

The sound bank replied…

'Male.'

Dave asked...

'Are you old or young?'

Again, it replied...

'Old and worried but listening.'

Dave asked...

'What is your connection with this house?'
Immediately it replied...

'Died!' then... *'Dead!'*

Dave asked...

'Are you trying to tell me something bad happened to you?'
It replied once more...

'Exactly.'

The pyramid then lit up green and beeped. Dave continued with his questions...

'Are you trying to tell me you were killed?'

It replied again…

'I am.'

Riley then asked…

'Do you know how you were killed?'

The spirit replied…

'Loose chair', then… *'Sorry.'*

Dave asked…

'Who did it?'

It replied…

'She's here!'

The next few words we heard weren't very clear, but we thought we heard that the male spirit was hit over the head and hurt his neck.

I asked out…

'Were you married?'

Dave backed me up and asked again as we got no answer from my attempt.

'Were you man and wife?'

The spirit said...

'Why?'

Dave continued...

'It's a simple question, simple answer?'

The spirit answered...

'No!'

Riley asked...

'Were you partners?'

It answered in a spooky drawn-out voice...

'Yes.'

I asked...

'Did you live here together?'

Dave thought he heard it say...

'Keep your nose out!'

Riley smiled and said, 'That's the second time I've heard it say that this evening.'

Three devices in the corner then screamed out alarms as if once again someone was standing there.

Dave asked out again...

'Can you tell me how many spirits are in this house?'
I didn't hear the answer to this, but Riley who was standing next to me did.

He asked...

'Could you confirm that number for me?'

The spirit definitively said...

'Three!'

Dave asked...

'The one who's speaking with us, are you the one that has been going up and down the stairs?'

The voice responded...

'It's a male.'

Another spirit appeared to join us as the voice was quite different from before.

It said...

'I'm here with you.'

The Aeroflux on the floor behind the table went off.

Riley asked...

'Did you die in the house?'

This reply was quite hard to hear but it sounded like it responded with...

'Leave him alone!'

Dave asked...

'Is there a woman in here?'

It responded…

'Yes!'

He then said…

'You are nothing to do with this house though, are you?'
The spirit responded…

'Visiting.'

Dave queried again…

'Where are you from?'

The spirit immediately said…

'Tram' followed by… *'I am dead!'*

Dave asked me if there was a tram line anywhere nearby. I informed him that there was one about one hundred and fifty yards behind my house.

He looked at me in amazement and as he was about to continue, she said again…

'Just visiting.'

Dave explained to me that there were three spirits here, a male on the stairs, the female from the tram stop and an older female. The older female had been with us all night and been watching on as we carried out the investigation. She had a real strong presence. As Dave was telling me this a voice came through saying…

'That's true!'

I started making coffees for the whole team as Dave asked…

'Can you give me an age for the person on the stairs?'

The spirit came through saying…

'Thirty-five.'

Dave then asked…

'Can you say my name? I've introduced myself tonight. In fact, can you say all four of our names?'

The spirit replied…

'Will, Riley, Kevin and Dave.'

Just after saying our names, we heard the REM pod on the stairs go off. Then the spirits voice said...

'Tell him, David.'

Dave mentioned that throughout the night he kept hearing the name 'Craig' come through and asked if there was any relevance. I explained that the strange thing is, the only person I know called Craig was the first person to see the old lady in the bay window before I moved in. Being a work colleague, he'd never actually been in the house but obviously knew of its whereabouts and of Mrs Tompkins.

As I was still making the coffees for the team Riley asked out...

'Spirit, have you seen me before?'

It replied...

'Yes!'

This made sense as he'd been here plenty of times before... mainly for the poker nights.

Dave reset the carbon monoxide device as it was now at the top of the scale in the red and could go no further. After resetting it stayed in the green and hardly moved. We all then heard another loud bang upstairs.

As the guys packed up the equipment from the kitchen, I asked how it had been for them so far. Dave replied, 'It's not been a bad night. I wouldn't say it's been eccentric so far, but you definitely have three spirits in the house with you.' I then left the room to go and grab the laptop to see if we'd managed to capture any noises from the hallway upstairs while we were downstairs in the far end of the building. The results were astounding.

The recording was only on for eight minutes which is strange, almost as though somebody had stopped the recording. I knew this was impossible as I was the last one to leave the laptop upstairs before joining the crew in the kitchen. I placed the laptop on the kitchen table and all four of us gathered round. I hit 'play'. We could all see the sound waves and hear me walking off down the stairs at the beginning of the recording to join the team for the investigation. Then in the next eight minutes I managed to capture four disembodied voices. I was unsure what three of the voices said but two were female and the other male. The fourth one clearly said, 'Hey!', and it was very loud as if someone was leaning towards the microphone on the laptop. Also, a male spirit could be heard coughing and two sets of separate footsteps at different times which coincided with the footsteps we'd heard whilst downstairs. The final recording was of a door slamming, which again we'd heard from downstairs.

The four of us, amazed at what we'd just heard from the laptop went to sit in the front room. I'd set the laptop up at the top of the stairs and hit 'record' again and Kevin went to the top of the stairs with a small handheld voice recorder to see if he could capture anything. On his return we sat in silence to listen back to the recording. There was nothing there to be heard. The house had gone quiet. You could hear a pin drop.

I grabbed the laptop after half an hour of silence and before we listened to the second recording, Dave shut his eyes to see if he could pick up on anything. After a minute or so he opened his eyes, looked at me and said, 'Do you ever hear a sewing machine, because I've just heard one?' I explained that wasn't something I'd heard before but it was strange that he should say that because the old lady used to work as a furrier making fur coats. Perhaps he was tuning in and hearing that.

The team left the house at around 12.45am and

as they left, I asked Dave again, 'So what do you think?' He looked at me and said, 'To be fair, we've had the devices going off all night, the three spirits coming through to talk to us and then the recordings you've captured. You've definitely got three powerful spirits. I wouldn't be surprised if you see them, or you see them move things within the house. It's up there with one of the most haunted properties I've visited in my time, not because of the number of spirits but what they can do.' With that final word they left me alone in the house.

We didn't get a chance to listen to the second recording, so I sat at the kitchen table after they'd left and was disappointed not to hear anything for the first twenty eight minutes apart from Kevin going upstairs to ask a few questions. I was just about to call it a night when I saw a few large sound waves coming up on the recording. I then heard through the laptop, a long-drawn-out voice which sounded like a woman humming or singing a playful melody and this was then followed by what sounded like something being thrown at a wall and bouncing on the floor. Both of these noises were captured only five minutes before the team had left and it's strange to think that all four of us were sitting in the front room below where the laptop was situated on the hallway at the top of the stairs, and we hadn't heard either of these noises. I left the laptop on the table and went back upstairs to check if there was anything on the floor. Not a thing. This was another implausible noise that had been captured on my recording device.

That night after the team left and I'd listened to the recordings, I walked up to my bedroom and turned the light on. I could hear noises outside the bedroom door. Had the house suddenly come back to life? The little amount of sleep I had that night was done with the light on and the TV in the bedroom playing to itself to drown out any noises. I certainly wasn't going to be communicating with any more spirits that night.

As I've mentioned before I am quite the sceptic but very open minded when it comes to the strange things I've seen with my own eyes and the paranormal events that have happened to friends and loved ones at number 333.

The investigation that unfolded on the 2nd of July 2022 was a verification to me of what I already thought was happening in the house. I kind of knew there was a male and a female spirit here as so many people have seen Mrs Tompkins, and the footsteps which are heard throughout the house always sounded like a heavy-set male figure. What I wasn't expecting was that we had a female visitor called Shelley who was something

to do with the local tram stop.

I had my own night vision camera set up in the front room on a small coffee table facing the door to the bottom of the stairs, as there had been so much paranormal activity in this area over the years. A week after the investigation I sat watching the two hours of footage, hoping to catch the door handle move or the shadowy figure pass the underside of the closed door. Neither of these things happened, however I did catch a ghostly male voice which seemed to whisper into the microphone of the camera... *'Be quiet.'*

This chilling voice wasn't heard on the night by the team or me as we were all in the far side of the kitchen extension at the time. However, the spirit which spoke said these words just before Dave can be heard speaking in the background saying, 'Come on spirits, you've gone quiet.' Upon hearing the voice, I phoned my dad to come round and listen on the headphones to get his thoughts on what it said, and we both came to the definite conclusion that it was a male whispering into the camera... *'Be quiet.'*

I am grateful to the team from 'Awakening the Paranormal'. Their use of numerous devices certainly showed that there must have been

THE LADY IN THE BAY WINDOW

some powerful unknown energy throughout the house. The sceptic in me questioned the two 'apps' within the phones which were placed on the table, but there is no doubt after listening back to the video recording that pretty much all the questions that were asked by the team, were intelligently answered by a spirit through the 'app'. I know as well as anybody that any 'app' or computer program can be made to do anything you want it to, but this was real and a proper head turner for a sceptic like me. The most amazing result was when Dave asked for the spirit to say our names and one by one it said them back to us through the 'app'.

After all this, the real icing on the cake was capturing real time noises from upstairs on the laptop. As I mentioned all the windows and doors were shut upstairs, the heating was off as it was the middle of summer, and no electrical devices were left on upstairs apart from the laptop which captured the noises.

I listened back to these noises through a 3D headset, and you can clearly hear footsteps walking along the hallway past the laptop from left to right and then later in the recording they go from right to left. This confirmed the fact that I've heard these footsteps for the past eighteen years. The footsteps are never in the same room as you and if you try to follow the noise it just stops. Maybe one day it won't stop, and I'll finally catch a glimpse of one of the three spirits that often haunt my house. For now, as long as they are happy, I'm happy to share this place with them.

The one recording that I've listened to the most is the object being thrown. It seems to be poltergeist activity and the kind of noise you could imagine hearing if a TV remote was thrown hard at a wall and then bounced across the floor. There was no one there to throw anything and nothing on the floor. What could this have been? If one of the spirits could throw something at that force, what else could it do?

TIM DOYLE - SPIRITUALIST MEDIUM INVESTIGATION

I'd been given Tim's details via a local spiritualist church. He came highly recommended as the medium who should investigate number 333. As with the paranormal group before him I didn't want to give away my name or address before the visit. Tim knew me only by the name Mr. G and I'd given him the first three digits of my postcode. I told him to phone me when he was close, so I could guide him to the property.

Tim arrived shortly after 5pm on Friday the 5th of August 2022 and duly phoned me as arranged. I was waiting at the front door to welcome him. We shook hands and I led him into the kitchen and asked if he would be ok with me filming and voice recording the whole conversation. Tim was more than happy with this and proceeded to tell me how this would all work.

He asked if there was a cellar, to which I replied there wasn't. Then he asked if there was an attic. I do have an attic, but it's only used for storage. Tim then told me that the spirits would guide him around the house to different rooms and we would have to follow at their command.

I asked…

'Would you like me to tell you where the paranormal hotspots have been?'

Tim replied…

'No, it's fine, the spirits will show me.'

Tim took a seat at the table in the kitchen and as I poured him a glass of water, he said…

'I've already picked up the name Jim, but I don't know who he is as yet.'

I took a seat across from Tim and set up the camera and voice recorder. Tim could clearly see the house had been renovated as we were currently sitting in the newly built extension.

He asked…

'Have you refurbished the house yourself and how long have you lived here?'

I told Tim that I'd lived here for eighteen years and the whole house had been renovated in this time.

Tim said...

'This could have a bearing on what is happening here. I'm not saying it does, but it could confuse spirits that have lived here before.'

Tim, looking cautiously around the room asked...

'So, what's going on here spirits in this house?'

He paused and made a throaty noise...

'This is weird, I seem to be picking up on a ship. I don't know if that's connected to you or the house but I'm seeing an old-fashioned ship,'

I then said...

'Sorry to ask this but how does this all work. I mean how do you communicate with spirits and pick up on things?'

Tim replied...

'We see in our mind's eye, we see, and we hear. I also link up with my spirit guides or any spirits that are here and talk with them through these means... I'm still being shown a ship, you wouldn't expect that here in the middle of England, maybe near the coast but not here.'

Tim asked if this could be to do with my family. It didn't ring any bells with me, but I did mention my grandad used to be in the Airforce. Could this be related?

Tim then mentioned that some messages that come through aren't always as clear as night and day. He said that most of the spirits that come through quite strongly are people who passed away whilst having unfinished business. These are the spirits which are closest to the earth's plane and tend to also be the most mischievous. Tim then told me that he could sometimes help these spirits through spirit counselling or as some people called it house cleansing. I proceeded to tell Tim that I didn't feel like it's the kind of haunting which is scary to me. I've been shocked by a few things that have happened to myself and others but if he were to communicate with any previous homeowners, I didn't want them to go, unless they wanted his help to move on.

Tim then took a breath and said...

'As soon as you said something shocked you, I was shown a door handle coming down and a door opening. Have you witnessed this happen with nobody around?'

Looking a little startled, I replied...

'That's the only thing I have seen with my own eyes.'

I didn't tell Tim about any of the incidents in the house prior to his visit, the only thing he knew he was coming to do, was a reading on the house. Not too long back a coin had been thrown at me, but I didn't see it until after it had hit me, I didn't reveal this information to Tim at the time.

Tim reckoned that whenever a door opened in front of me, it could be a message for me, like a metaphor for a door opening in my life to an opportunity.

He then said...

'Would you understand Ernest?'

I replied...

'No.'

I didn't know anybody called Ernest; however, I've spoken with my mum since and Ernest was my grandad's older brother on my mum's side.

Tim then asked if I knew any history of the house, to which I replied...

'Yes, bits… not everything as it's been quite hard to find.'

Tim then asked something which made me laugh…

'Did you once think of getting the TV spiritualist medium, Derek Acorah, into the house?'

I laughed because it had always been a standing joke between the lads and me. They'd always said I should get Derek Acorah in to have a chat with the spirits that were causing the paranormal events around the house. I explained that I was quite a sceptic but also open-minded to what had gone on over the years, as too many things had happened for me to turn a blind eye. I also told Tim that the whole paranormal world intrigued me, and that I did watch the odd paranormal investigation on TV. Tim told me that the spirits in the house had heard Derek's name mentioned before and wanted to let me know that they knew I was going to get someone in at some stage to try and communicate with them.

Tim then asked if I had a lump on my stomach or hernia. I did a couple of years back have a painful lump just above my groin which I'd seen a doctor about. This shocked me a little as nobody knew about this. It turned out to be a twisted muscle, kind of like a hernia but something that sorted itself out over the following months.

Tim received a message from the spirits that they wanted us to walk around the house. We both stood up from the table, and I followed Tim through the kitchen and into the front room. He walked with his hands outstretched around the room seeing if he could feel a presence, he then asked...

'Have you heard a song being sung?'

I replied...

'Actually, very recently I set my laptop up at the top of the stairs during a paranormal investigation and had captured a lady's voice humming or singing a melody.'

Tim continued to walk with his arms outstretched. His right hand came to settle just below head height as if he were tapping somebody on the head.

'There's a boy here and he's telling me he's here most of the time. He didn't live here but he's resting here. He's showing me that he's shovelling coal into the fireplace which must have been here.'

Tim pointed to where the old fireplace used to be, which is now a plain wall with the corner sofa covering what would have housed the fireplace. Tim was still communicating with the boy to find out more when he said...

'He's showing me back to the war times, World War Two. I can see bombs coming down.'

It's well documented that Sheffield was heavily bombarded by the Germans in World War Two, and it was called the Sheffield Blitz, in which many lives were lost and properties severely damaged.

'He says he's just playing with you, whetting your appetite, not trying to scare you but knows that you are interested in the spirit world and wants to show you what he can do. He knows a lot about you. He's showing me your mum, she's been long suffering with cancer, and he knows it's playing on your mind. He's saying you need to sort your right knee out; you have a problem and it's not getting better.'

I put on a brave face and smiled as the information the spirit was telling me through Tim was spot on. These are things he really couldn't have known. I do worry about my mum daily, and I'd recently been told that I need a replacement right knee, though being too young I'd have to wait until I'm forty five to have the surgery carried out. I'd been on the phone with the doctor that morning to book in for my next steroid injection in my knee, as the pain was getting worse by the day.

Tim then said...

'This lad says he wants to follow us round the house and tell us things along the way as he knows everything about you.'

He then asked...

'Do you have a lady friend?'

I said...

'Yes, I'm married.'

Tim replied...

'She's feeling really tired at the minute and needs to go to the doctors to get this sorted.' I nodded. This was another indicator to me that the boy did indeed know my wife and me. She was booked in for the following week to speak with the doctors about a current medical condition. He told me we really needed to take this seriously and get it sorted.

The spirits then asked Tim to follow him back into the kitchen where he picked up the names Arthur and Sean. The names didn't mean anything to me but could have been something to do with the house. Tim then picked up that the spirits were showing him an old Bedford van that had something to do with Arthur and his job as a carpet fitter. There's also a lady here by the name of June, she's asking if you've heard a clicking sound. This is her knitting. She loves to knit and make clothing. She also uses a mangle to dry her clothes and you may have heard it. I've heard many a strange noise throughout the house and looking back, one of the noises we hear does sound like two knitting needles clicking together. I asked if Tim could pick up any surnames as the historical documents I had, didn't have first names, just surnames. Tim immediately picked up the name 'Brown'. I was struggling to find any relevance to the house with this name.

Tim and I walked upstairs, and he was drawn straight to the first closed door which was the master bedroom. Tim looking slightly concerned said...

'I can see a vortex in here, that's basically where spirits can come in from one dimension to another. These things are a bit like a wormhole for people who have passed. The portal is usually used in the early hours of the morning, that's when you'll hear most of the rush of energy of spirits coming through. They aren't all staying here, they are using the vortex to enter and then moving on to other local homes.'

Tim left the room and entered Elliot's room. He asked...

'Is your son oblivious to everything that's going

on?'

I smiled and replied...

'Yes, he hasn't really got a clue as he's a seventeen-year-old lad who spends most of his time with his headset on, playing games with his mates on his computer.'

Tim then said...

'The spirits tend to leave him alone, but they are aware of him. They just don't want to scare him. A lot of the spirits in the house aren't residents, but just passing through.'
Tim looked out of the second bedroom window on to the rear garden and said...

'Where's the shed gone?'

I explained that there used to be a shed in the garden in the place he was pointing. He then said...

'Someone's not happy that their shed has gone.'

We continued into the bathroom where Tim stood for a while before picking anything up. Someone then came through...

Then Tim said *'I'm sorry, I didn't mean to break down.* It's a lady. She's quite well built and very upset. She hanged herself. She took her own life.

Are you related to the property? he asked.

'No...'

Do you live here?

'No...'

What's your name?

'Mary McGill.'

'She's in her forties and she worked up the road.'

Tim then looked up and asked...

'Have you had any writing, as in writing on the walls? She's saying she does the writing... it's not on the walls sorry... it's in a diary, she's showing me she had a diary. Do you do anything in this house to make yourself known?

'No...'

'Who does?'

'It's the boy.'

She's showing me a ball rolling across a floor. This could be symbolic... have you seen something move across the floor or had anything thrown or moved?'

Not wanting to give the game away I said...

'Yes, things have happened, but I want to see if they will tell you what they are, as opposed to you hearing it from me.'

Tim then said...

'I have to give you the name Tom, it's quite a common name but this one is relating to you.'

At the time I was unaware that my mum's grandad was called Tom and he'd actually come back in spirit form to speak with my mum on the night before she married my dad. This was the first and only time my mum had ever had a visit from a spirit.

Tim walked into my office and said he could see an

overhead projector. He asked me if I owned an old projector for showing old photos and things.

I replied...

'My dad has one of those, it used to be his dad's. My grandad used to show us all his old photos a long time ago. I think it's currently stored in my mum and dad's loft.'

Tim then walked back into the master bedroom and said...

'There's something to do with this bay window, a girl. She's only around twelve years old and has a very pointy chin and plump cheeks. She's smiling and saying she's just here for the ride. She often uses the vortex like a large kids' slide to arrive in your bedroom and go to visit her local family. This vortex is used by over a hundred spirits. There are vortexes like this all over the country.'

I asked...

'When you walked in you said there was something about this bay window, what can you tell me about that?'

Tim replied...

'When I walked in the spirits showed me an image of the bay window from the outside, I'm not sure why?'

Deep down I knew why, that's where the spirit of Mrs Tompkins had been seen twice before but again, I didn't want to give the game away, so I didn't mention this to Tim.

As we walked back downstairs, Tim asked why I had a laptop set up on the stairs. I explained to him that when the paranormal team had been in, we'd managed to pick up many different sounds including footsteps.

Tim asked me to take him to the door handle which had opened by itself. He grabbed the handle and closed his eyes before shouting...

'Get out! Get out! Get out of my house!'

'Oh, this is not a nice spirit. He doesn't want us here. He's telling me he's the owner.'

'You were the owner, but you aren't anymore.'

Tim pointed at me and said...

'This is that gentleman's house.'

Tim continued…

'Keith Howes, that's his name. Why do you keep coming back? Ah ok, you are looking for your wife, sorry your partner. This one seems very upset, very direct. Would you like me to send him on and help him?'

I replied…

'I'm more than happy if he wants to go, please help him.'

Tim then said…

'Ok Keith, I'm going to help you find your partner. If you look around the room, you will see a light coming from me and one from this gent to the side of me. Look beyond those lights and you will see a real bright light, the brightest one you can see. If you walk towards it, you will see a hand and that hand is showing you the way to love, peace and tranquillity. Now go to it, use my energy. God bless you… he just said, *thank you.*'

At this stage the battery on my camera went dead. A fully charged battery which should last two hours had lasted less than one hour.

We both walked into the kitchen as I poured Tim another glass of water. It was thirty degrees outside and the four bifold doors were fully open onto the rear garden. At this stage I explained to Tim that my name was William and the reason I'd asked him to come was that I was writing a book about all the paranormal events which had happened in my home over the years. I had to explain this as I didn't want to use Tim's name for the book without his permission. We both sat at the table as the discussion continued.

I asked...

'Out of interest, I noticed you grabbed the door handle to pick up on something. Could you try this with a couple of objects I have?'

Tim said he'd be more than happy to try. First, I handed him a pool ball. This pool ball had mysteriously appeared as an extra ball when I was playing pool with my good friend Dan (aka the Captain) just one week before he passed away. He pocketed the ball on the night in question and said he would keep it as his lucky ball because it had the number thirteen on it, which as we all know is unlucky for some. He gave me the ball the next day and said, 'Keep it, you need luck more than me.' I've kept the pool ball in my bedside table ever since his passing.

Tim picked up the ball and said...

'This is a strange one, I'm getting the name Darren, and another spirit that is really overshadowing me. Do you understand a brawl in a bar?'

This didn't relate to the ball but was Tim picking up on the fact my brother Darren was known for causing the odd scuffle in local pubs.

I replied...

'No', as I didn't think at the time the two were related.

Tim then continued...

'I don't know why but I'm seeing someone with their arms up in the air like they are at a concert or gig, something like Glastonbury. Is this a bit raw or a bit fresh?'

I replied...

'It probably always will be a little fresh. It was my

THE LADY IN THE BAY WINDOW

best mate's, and he gave it me a week before he passed, does that help?'

He then said…

'I'm getting shown a pickaxe.'

That's a term I had been referred to in the past by Dan as a nickname.

Tim then said…

'I don't know why but he's not speaking to me, he's just showing me images. He's showing me a pain on his head and he's now speaking saying it wasn't intentional. He's telling me what happened to him shouldn't have happened, but he was trying something… a recreational drug and it wasn't right, it was a lot stronger than it should have been. But he's ok, he's showing me a festival again, waving his arms around.'

I sat motionless. I felt an overwhelming sadness come over me that this was Dan trying to communicate but I also felt happy that he sounded like he was having a blast at a festival, which looking back was his favourite thing to do. I pulled myself together and passed Tim the three American one cent coins which had appeared randomly a few months prior.

Tim asked...

'Do you know someone American?'

I replied...

'Yes, a good friend lives in America with his American partner.'

Tim then said...

'I believe these are to do with him or his partner. As in a spirit is trying to show themselves to you, so you can tell them...' Tim then paused midsentence.

'...Simon. Can you ask them if they know a Simon and let them know that he's ok? He's not coming through very strong but that's all I'm getting.'

This name didn't mean anything to me. However, I did speak with Paul, who is the friend who lives in the States, the following week. He told me he didn't know anybody called Simon. He then spoke with his partner Sandy who said, 'This is a little freaky but a good friend of mine lost his dog not too long back and it was called Simon.'

I asked Tim if there were any more spirits that wanted to say anything while he was here.

He said...

'I'm feeling a female coming through on your mum's side, her name begins with an M, Margaret, something like that. But I can't see her. Were you not close to your grandma?

I replied...

'I am still close with my nannan. She's still around.'

Tim said...

'That's why I can't see her, but for some reason I'm being told about her. I'm getting the name Tom again, he's quite a strong presence with you.'

I never knew Tom, my great grandad, so didn't have much to say.

Tim then said...

'He's pinning a medal on you, as if to say you are doing well. He wishes you well with the book and he's showing me a book signing. He says it's going to be a success and you will achieve more than you think. Don't lose faith, you will come across some issues getting it out there, but everything will pan out alright and this may be a steppingstone to other things.'

Tim asked if there was anything else I would like to ask.

I asked…

'How many spirits would you say are residents here?'

Tim took his time and said…

'I'm speaking with an elderly lady now, she's got grey, shortish hair and she's telling me there are four spirits who reside here.'

I asked…

'Can you see what she is wearing?'

Tim then said…

'She is probably in her seventies at least and she's

wearing a skirt, a blouse and a cardigan.'

I asked Tim if he could get me a name, he came back with Mary. He didn't manage to get a surname.

I asked…

'Can you tell me what sort of job she had?'

He said…

'She's showing me a sweet factory like Liquorice Allsorts. I don't think that was her only job though, she's taking me down the Moor in Sheffield but I'm not quite sure what she's doing.'

I also found this really strange as my nannan, did actually work for Bassetts Liquorice Allsorts before she retired.

That concluded my time with Tim Doyle the spiritualist medium. In some ways this left me with more questions to the endless mysteries of number 333. I do however feel he may have picked up on Mrs Tompkins right at the end of the reading. The description matches that of all the sightings over the years.

It's now been 8 months since Tim visited me at my home. The strange occurrences have continued, and I've finally caught something strange on CCTV outside the house. Over this time, I've done five drafts of the book and am just about to send the finished article to a few close family and friends to help with the final edit.

As I said at the beginning of the book, I'm not a writer but I just felt I needed to document and share my paranormal experiences. This in turn would help me to raise money for a local cancer charity. So if you have enjoyed reading about the many spooky stories of my home, tell your friends and family to go online and buy the book. The more sales, the more money raised.

After all this, I still call myself a sceptic with an open mind... I've seen and heard too much. Maybe one day Mrs Tompkins will appear before me and fully change my mind.

For my Mum

1957 - 2023

My mum sadly never got a chance to read the final published version of the book. I know how proud she was that I'd taken it upon myself to write my story to raise money for her chosen charity, Cavendish Cancer Care, who helped my mum throughout her diagnosis and treatment.

I dedicate this book to you. I love you and hope we will be together again one day.

THANK YOU FOR READING MY BOOK.

If you would like to find out more information about 'The Lady in the Bay Window' please search for it on Facebook. I'd love to hear from you. Feel free to drop me a message or simply leave me a review on either Amazon or the Facebook page.

If you would like to find out more about Cavendish Cancer Care and the services they provide, please visit:
https://cavcare.org.uk/about-us/

Made in the USA
Coppell, TX
16 November 2023